Siena, Italy

The History of the City, a Travel Guide for Tourism

Author
Roman Reynolds.

SONITTEC PUBLISHING. All rights reserved. No part of this publication may be reproduced, distributed, or transmitted in any form or by any means, including photocopying, recording, or other electronic or mechanical methods, without the prior written permission of the publisher, except in the case of brief quotations embodied in critical reviews and certain other noncommercial uses permitted by copyright law. For permission requests, write to the publisher, addressed "Attention: Permissions Coordinator," at the address below.

Copyright © 2019 Sonittec Publishing
All Rights Reserved

First Printed: 2019.

Publisher:
SONITTEC LTD
College House, 2nd Floor
17 King Edwards Road,
Ruislip
London
HA4 7AE

Table of Content

- **SUMMARY** 1
- **INTRODUCTION** 9
- **HISTORY** 12
- **SIENA TOURISM** 17
  - TRAVEL GUIDE 17
    - Siena and Touristic Importance 25
    - Montalcino, Siena Travel Guide 28
    - Monteriggioni, Siena Travel Guide 36
    - Palio di Siena Travel Guide 42
    - Piazza del Campo, Siena Travel Guide 49
    - Piccolomini Library, Siena Travel Guide 54
    - Santa Maria della Scala Travel Guide 60
    - San Gimignano Travel Guide 74
    - Monuments In Siena 82
    - Museums In Siena 86
    - Parks & Gardens In Siena 91
    - Le Fonti Di Siena 93
    - Excursions Around Siena 95
    - Travels In Tuscany 99
    - Walking & Bike Tours In Siena 103
    - Itineraries In Siena 104
    - Thermal Springs In Siena 109
    - Terre Di Siena 111
      - Chianti, Tuscany 111
      - Crete Senesi 113
      - Monte Amiata 119
      - Val Di Chiana 122
      - Val D'elsa 128
      - Val D'orcia 133
      - Val Di Merse 139
    - Restaurants In Siena 147
      - Top Spots For Aperitivo In Siena 155
    - Transportation In Siena 160
      - To Get in 160
      - To Get around 163
    - Weather In Siena 165
    - Shopping in Siena 166
    - Sports In Siena 173
    - Theaters In Siena 176
    - Nightlife In Siena 178
    - Quality Of Life In Siena 181
    - Events In Siena 182
    - Etruscans Of Siena 185

Summary

Why You should Travel More, when there are so Many Benefits of Traveling!

Everyone keeps saying how important it is to travel. So what's all this fuss about?
The benefits of traveling are not just a one-time thing: traveling changes you physically and psychologically. Having little time or money isn't a valid excuse. You can fly for cheap very easily. If you have a full-time job and a family, you can still travel on the weekends or holidays, even with a baby.

Here are some of the main benefits of traveling. And I'm sure that once you get started, you'll find some more yourself!

Traveling Improves Your Health
From cutting down on stress, to lowering your chances of developing a heart disease, the health benefits of traveling are huge. You may stay sitting on a chair all day long at the workplace: including some walking to your trip is sure to make

your body feel better. For some people, wandering abroad is even a cure for depression and anxiety. Of course, it's not a foolproof cure, but it might help you feel better, both physically and psychologically.

Traveling more is likely to have a tremendous impact on your mental well-being, especially if you're no used to going out of your comfort zone. Trust me: travel more and your doctor will be happy. Be sure to get in touch with your physician, they might recommend some medication to accompany you in your travels, especially if you're heading to regions of the globe with potentially dangerous diseases.

Traveling Disconnects You From Your Daily Life
This is extremely related to my previous point. We tend to be so caught up in our daily lives that sometimes by simply sticking around we may cause more harm than good. Your boss is taking over your life? Kids are driving you mad? Your parents are trying to make you live the life they want? How long do you think you can handle this pressure before you burst and everything falls apart?

Sometimes it is best to take a step back, take a deep breath and take go that Tower Bridge selfie. In all seriousness, travel is not a bad option - it is the most natural way of inducing the feeling you miss someone or that you are missed. The trick is to leave with a bit of preparation to avoid making a mistake during your journey. Plus, if you're flying, you better start thinking about booking your tickets sooner than later.

Traveling Makes You Smarter
Get used to picking up new words in a different language every time you travel and you will see improvements in your brain capacities, as Dan Roitman wrote in the Huffington Post. If only this, start getting familiar with travel jargon.

Even more than "just" languages, traveling helps you learn about yourself. You might run into challenging situations where you need to be resourceful and think differently. I'm sure that you will develop a new set of skills that you didn't suspect you had within you.

Traveling Improves Your Understanding of Other Cultures
Being more understanding and tolerant about a culture different than ours is part of being smarter, but I consider it as a benefits of traveling in itself. There is a quote by Saint Augustine, which goes "The world is a book, and those who do not travel read only one page". You could think of it this way: if you read what's in the news or watch the news on TV and don't

question it, you're missing on a ton of information. You might think that it makes you smarter and more aware of the world, but it's the exact opposite: it narrows your mind to a unique and biased perspective.

Sure, you probably feel comfortable where you are, but that is just a fraction of the world! If you are a student, take advantage of programs such as Erasmus to get to know more people, experience and understand their culture. Dare traveling to regions you have a skeptical opinion about. I bet that you will change your mind and realize that everything is not so bad abroad.

Traveling Makes You More Interesting
I have no doubt that you're quite the conversationalist. That being said, including a few stories from abroad is likely to grant you even more attention. Mentioning something that most people aren't familiar with or bring a new perspective is always a good way to shine in a social situation.

Who do you think people want to listen to: the guy who spent his vacations at home doing some gardening and reading the newspaper, or the one who spent a week in Cuba, driving an old American car, swimming with dolphins and tasting deliciously spicy food? I know which story I want to hear about...

Traveling Allows You to try Amazing Food
Speaking of food, I bet you're one hell of a chef and your home meals are delicious. But there is no such thing as trying a typical local dish from another country. Don't trick yourself into going to the Sushi shop next door: you don't know what sushi tastes like until you've been to Japan.

Eating local food in a new country is an entirely new experience. All the flavors are different. Here me out: I'm French and I love our local recipes. You do to. But let's not kid ourselves: some change would be more than welcome in our daily diet. If only because we're naturally curious. Some food bloggers travel thousands of kilometers for a specific dish! The least you can do is travel to the next region and try something new.

Traveling Makes You Feel Like an Adventurer
Despite the fact that the world has never been as well connected as today, there are still places that are little known to the average tourist. Setting up a list of places you want to visit is extremely motivating. You have something tangible to go after. I'm currently working on my own bucket list, and I

think I'll never see the end of it, with all these amazing destinations.

The benefit of traveling to a new place is that it forces you to face the unknown and think differently. You don't need to go spend a month in the jungle! If you live in a large city, just going on a hike over the weekend will make you feel different. Adventures require novelty, so get out of your comfort zone. It might be scary, but in retrospect, you'll see it as the best decision you ever made!

Traveling Expands Your (Real) Social Network
Believe it or not, social networks was once like a real thing - in real life. Crazy, I know. Establishing connections and building a network abroad is one of the smartest things you can do in today's world. It is sometimes hard to build long-lasting relationship with the people you meet abroad, but it doesn't mean it's not worth meeting new people!

Take this example: I've spent last year's New Year's Eve in Tanzania. I slept for two days at the flat of an Egyptian expat. I met him on Couchsurfing, once of the best ways to find cheap accommodation when you travel. Now, a year later, this guy invites me to his wedding in Egypt! How amazing is that?!

Some connections you make over your travels are surprisingly strong.

Traveling Creates Lifetime Memories
My grandfather was an amazing story-teller and he used to tell me stories of the trips he made when he was younger. One of my favorites is how he tried eating with chopsticks in China for the first time. He regretted not traveling more as a young man. Years later, he still remembered everything in details: because traveling made a real impression on him. And it probably will on you too.

No matter how insignificant it may seem, the fact that you've had an experience abroad, something that was out of the ordinary, creates a memory that you will remember for a long time.

Traveling Makes You Love Your Home Even More
"The magic thing about home is that it feels good to leave, and it feels even better to come back". You will truly understand the meaning of those words by Wendy Wunder, only upon your return home. On the one hand, it would seem that you're back where you started, same setting, same people, same problems. Yet you're not the same - you're new, full of new knowledge and ideas!

I know that I was getting bored after living my whole life in the same place. I needed to get out, I need a change of scene. I was focusing only the negative: how there isn't much to do around, how you always meet the same people, how nothing changes. Now, when I come home, I'm glad about all of this and I see only the positive..

Introduction

Gloriously Gothic and effortlessly civilised, intimate Siena is Tuscany's most seductive calling card. This compact, Italian city is endlessly intriguing, from the shell-shaped Campo to the galleries full of doe-eyed Madonnas and sad-eyed saints.

Born middle-aged, Siena is an antidote to fashion lists. It has smugly looked the same for 900 years and has no truck with trends. In essence, it's Italy's last surviving city-state: a provincial capital with the psychology of a village and the grandeur of a nation.

Siena is the counterpoint to nearby Florence. It's as medieval as its rival is Renaissance. It's the feminine foil to Florentine masculinity: Siena paints Madonnas; Florence prefers the machismo of Michelangelo's David.

Change is anathema to the Sienese, but what is there to alter? The rose-brick cityscape is too coherent to tweak. The locals have been giving lessons in living since the enlightened city council first set the tone in the 13th century. Its hearty food and wine still converts hardened sinners and the biannual Palio horse race continues to command the passion of the population.

Today, romantics drift along medieval alleys suffused with melancholy charm. Tall, flush-brick palaces conceal world-class art collections. Culture vultures slaver over the turreted town hall and the theatrical mansions. Mystical churches and monumental fountains are simply part of the furniture; quaffing Chianti and Brunello di Montalcino wines in the Medici Fortress an everyday joy. Tomorrow they might tour the vineyards by Vespa or take a Tuscan cookery course in a countryside kitchen. Carved into Etruscan cellars, the city's homely inns are full of foodies salivating over truffles and wild boar pasta.

Siena is a chiaroscuro city, from its striped marble Cathedral to its black-and-white city emblem. Tunnelled backstreets open into the brilliant, light-bathed Campo, where all roads eventually lead. Locals liken it to the enveloping cloak of the

Madonna, the city's patron saint, yet Italians know it as a city '*a misura d'uomo*' (a city 'made to the measure of man').

When your horizons shrink to a single neighbourhood bar, you will have discovered the Sienese spirit. It's time slow down and start walking.

History

Siena, city, central Italy, in the Toscana (Tuscany) regione. It lies about 30 miles (48 km) south of Florence. The city was important in history as a commercial and banking city until surpassed by Florence in the 13th–14th century.

The site of Siena was originally an Etruscan settlement that later became the Roman city of Sena Julia. This colony disappeared, but the new Siena that later developed flourished under the Lombard kings. In the 12th century it became a self-governing commune. Economic rivalry and territorial conflict with neighbouring Florence, which was anti-imperial, or Guelf, made Siena the centre of pro-imperial Ghibellinism in Tuscany. The Sienese reached the peak of political success on Sept. 4, 1260, when their army crushed the Florentines at the Battle of Montaperti.

Siena became an important banking centre in the 13th century but was unable to compete with its rival, Florence. The imperial cause declined, and the popes imposed economic sanctions against Siena's Ghibelline merchants. Soon afterward, Siena itself turned Guelf, and the Ghibelline nobility lost its share of power. The city suffered from wars and famines and from the general economic decline that afflicted Italy in the early 14th century, and it was also devastated by outbreaks of the Black Death, which began in 1348. Struggles for power between factions of nobles, merchants, and the people replaced the strife between Guelfs and Ghibellines but did little to give Siena internal stability.

Despite these problems, the Sienese maintained an overall prosperity that enabled them to embellish their city with beautiful churches, palaces, towers, and fountains. In the decades of economic and moraldepression following the Black Death, Siena entered an era of heightened religiosity, during which the city produced two renowned saints, Catherine and Bernardino. Siena retained its independence during the 15th century, but economic stagnation continued. In 1487 an exiled aristocrat, Pandolfo Petrucci, seized power and ruled with brutal tyranny through a period of French and Spanish invasions until his death in 1512. His regime was continued by his family until 1524. After a long and heroic defense, Siena surrendered to the Spaniards in 1555, and two years later Philip II of Spain ceded the city to Florence. In 1861 Siena, together with the rest of Tuscany, was absorbed into the new Kingdom of Italy.

Because Siena's building activity was largely suspended in the 16th century, and because most modern building has taken place outside the city walls, Siena's original character remains unspoiled, and Siena remains essentially a medieval town. The walls and gates enclose a city centre that is composed of narrow, winding streets and old buildings and palaces. The centre of the city is dominated by a large, shell-shaped square called the Piazza del Campo, which is the focus of Siena's civic life. Tourists come to Siena in large numbers to view the Corsa del Palio, the famous horse races of medieval origin that are held twice annually on the Piazza del Campo amid colourful festivities. Standing alongside the square is the massive Public Palace (Palazzo Pubblico; 1297–1310), which is the seat of civil government. The interior of the Public Palace is decorated by works of the great masters of Sienese painting, including the "Maestà" of Simone Martini and frescoes by Ambrogio

Lorenzetti. The palace also contains the remains of the Gaia Fountain, which was one of the finest fountains carved by the Sienese sculptor Jacopo della Quercia. To one side of the Public Palace rises the slender, 334-foot (102-metre) bell tower known as the Mangia Tower (1338–48). Among the city's other impressive palaces are those of the Tolomei, Buonsignori, Sansedoni, and Salimbeni.

Siena's great cathedral was begun in the 12th century in the Romanesque style but was transformed in the 13th century into one of the finest examples of Italian Gothic. The walls and columns of the church's interior are covered with black and white marble, and its marble floors have decorative inlays by Domenico Beccafumi. Pinturicchio painted frescoes for the Piccolomini Library, which adjoins the cathedral and which was founded in 1495 by Cardinal Francesco Piccolomini, who later became Pope Pius III. A magnificent baptismal font with bas-reliefs by Jacopo della Quercia, Donatello, and Lorenzo Ghiberti distinguishes the Church of San Giovanni, which serves as the crypt for the cathedral.

Siena produced some of the greatest Italian painters of the 13th and 14th centuries; many masterpieces by Duccio di

Buoninsegna, Simone Martini, Pietro and Ambrogio Lorenzetti, and Sassetta are found in Siena's art gallery (in the Buonsignori Palace) as well as in the Public Palace and the Museum of Works of the Duomo. The latter museum also contains Duccio's great "Maestà," which was painted (1308–11) to celebrate the Sienese victory at Montaperti.

Siena was fortunate in escaping damage during World War II, and it now survives as a provincial town of great beauty and charm. It is also an archbishopric. The University of Siena was founded in 1240. The city has some light industry, but it is not on a major national highway or major rail route, although there is a road to Florence. Siena thrives on the visitors attracted by its artistic treasures and medieval monuments. It also serves as a market town for the surrounding agricultural area, which produces cattle, cereal grains, olives, and, above all, wines, its Chianti being perhaps the best known of all Italian wines. Pop. (2011) 52,839.

Siena Tourism
Travel Guide

Historical Siena is arranged around three radiating ridges of high ground, with green valleys enclosed within the old city walls. The town is divided into *terzi*, or thirds, and within each of these there are a number of the districts known as *contrade* (more about the *contrade* below). It's easy to walk around the historic centre of Siena on foot, exploring as you go, but if you're the organised type you may find it helpful to take the *terzi* one at a time.The Tourist Information Offices and museums supply leaflet guides to each one. The Terzo di Camollia, for example, contains the gigantic and shadowy Basilica di San Francesco, dating from the late 13th century; the rival Dominican church, the Basilica of San Domenico; the Sanctuary of St Catherine of Siena; the former Medici Fortress, which is now a pleasant and panoramic public park.

The first stop for tourists in Siena is Piazza del Campo (otherwise known simply as il Campo). This is the secular heart of Siena, a sloping amphitheatre of a square, lined with cafe tables and thronged with tourists, school parties and locals. The Campo is the dramatic setting for the Palio horserace. The piazza's focal point is the Palazzo Pubblico, the public palace, which dates back to 1250 and is still the seat of the Municipality.

The Palazzo is also home to some fine frescoes, and makes a good beginning to your sightseeing tour. At the ticket office in the internal courtyard you can buy a range of tickets. These give access to differing numbers of Siena's attractions, and some are valid for several days - a good way to save money, if you're planning a longer stay. A combined ticket gives you access to the Museo Civico inside the Palazzo, and also to the tall belltower, the Torre del Mangia. The tower is an excellent way to view Siena, the views over the town and countryside are breathtaking and help the visitor understand the geography of the town. Be warned though, that the climb is also breathtaking. A limited number of people are allowed up at a time, and you'll understand why when you see how narrow and poky the stairs are. The final climb up to the highest bell on its lofty framework is a nervewracking ladder - don't even think of making the climb if you have a poor head for heights or are very unfit.

Moving on to the museum, highlights include superb frescoes by Simone Martini, whose Maestà religious scene is one of the oldest examples of Sienese painting and glows with colour and life. Even more fascinating is a fresco cycle by Ambrogio Lorenzetti (1319-1348), the Allegories of Good and Bad Government. In one series, a 'good' ruler presides over a prosperous city (Siena) and productive countryside, while the effects of bad government are shown to be dismal misery and urban deprivation. Also worth seeing are an exquisite rose-tree made of gold (a gift to Siena from a pope), and some beautiful carved choir stalls with religious illustrations (one fine example shows the dead clambering from their graves on Judgement Day).

Heading uphill from the Campo, you arrive outside the monumental green-and-white-striped Duomo, Siena's cathedral. Before the collapse of the city's fortunes, Siena had ambitious plans to enlarge the edifice into the largest in the world. You can still see the facade and one side of the new cathedral, which would have incorporated the older building as a mere transept. Work was stopped, but the grandiose ambitions of the Sienese were preserved in the freestanding striped walls. The interior of the cathedral itself is ornate and decorated, lined with the heads of saints.

The floor is composed of extremely fine inlaid marble scenes - some are covered to preserve them from wear, but others are usually exposed in roped-off sections. The Duomo is free to visit; although there is a small charge to visit the Piccolomini Library, (off to the left of the nave), where charming courtly scenes by Pinturicchio recount the life story of Sienese Pope Enea Silvio Piccolomini (Pius II). Adjacent to the Duomo, the Museo dell'Opera Metropolitana contains much of the original artwork from the cathedral, Sienese paintings, and the opportunity to view Siena from a vantage point on the unfinished new cathedral facade.

Florence is one of the most popular tourist destinations in the Tuscan region of Italy, followed closely by Pisa, where the famous leaning tower can be found, and Cortona, which has gained a lot of fame via a movie starring Diane Lane. There is one Tuscan city however that some people fail to add to their list of go-to places when they come to this part of Italy, and that is Siena.

If you are into the Medieval Period, love gothic architecture, and want to take a step back into time while enjoying the best that the region has to offer, then Siena is one city you should not miss visiting. It is a scenic university town that is built upon three hills, and is surrounded by ancient walls, Chianti vineyards, and olive trees. Among its many attractions are well-preserved structures that date back to the 11th century. Walking around this city will make you feel that you have indeed traveled back in time.

Where to Go and What to See

Siena has a treasure trove of sights for you to see and interesting places for you to go to. When it comes to sightseeing, the number of age-old buildings you can marvel at here is rather astounding. Some of the most popular ones in the city include the following:

The Duomo
The Duomo di Siena is a church in the city that has been around since the medieval times. Also called the Siena Cathedral, this majestic edifice was designed and completed in the early to

mid-1200s, and was built on what actually is the former site of an old Roman temple. The cathedral showcases the marvelous talents of Renaissance and Medieval artists as well as architects such as Nicola Pisano, Pinturicchio, Giovanni Pisano, and Libreria Piccolomini. Other notable names that contributed to the grandeur and beauty of this structure include Michelangelo, Gian Lorenzo Bernini, and Donatello.

Piazza Del Campo

Also called Il Campo by locals, this piazza has been the social and civic center of Siena since the mid-12th century. It is also another popular structure built upon an old similar one, much like the Duomo, but this one is built on top of an old Roman marketplace. The piazza is a popular meeting place for locals and tourists alike, with the perimeter dotted with cafes where people can relax and watch the day go by as they chat with friends and acquaintances.

Pinacoteca Nazionale

Art lovers will definitely be enthralled by the Pinacoteca Nazionale, with its Renaissance and Medieval paintings by various Italian artists. The art pieces that you will find here include those made by Bartolo di Fredi, Simone Martini, and

Guido da Siena, to mention a few. This national gallery was first established in the early 1930s and is located in the Brigidi and Buonsignori palaces, which is located in the heart of the city. This gallery is said to have the largest collection of Sienese paintings that come with gold backgrounds, which are notably from the 14th and 15th century.

How to Get Around

Much like other places in Italy, the best way for you to enjoy this city is by foot. Walk around on the cobblestoned streets and marvel at the well-preserved ancient buildings around you. If you find that walking around all day is not your thing, you can actually go around in a Vespa, or any other scooter for that matter, to see and explore the city in a faster and easier manner.

Taking a car to Siena will only be more of a hassle than a convenience since you will need special permits to enter specific parts of the city with such a vehicle. You will also need to locate the parking lots in the city for you to be able to park your car without having to worry about fines, although there are a few street parking spaces that you can also park at. Parking rates are hourly, with day parking passes and 3-day parking passes also available for those who might be returning to these parking facilities frequently.

What to Do

Aside from the general sightseeing and tours, you might want to try experiencing events and activities that only happen in Siena. If you find yourself in this medieval city in July or August, you might want to check out the Palio di Siena, which is a bareback horserace that happens in honor of the Virgin Mary. You can also go on a wine tasting tour of some of the wineries nearby with expert guides and a select few tourists with the same love of wine as yourself.

You can also try to learn how to cook a few Tuscan dishes with cooking lessons in the city. Local chefs can teach you how to create some of the most well-known Tuscan favorites around, like bruschetta, pici, crostini, and hand-made pasta. Bring home more than just memories of this majestic ancient city and surprise family as well as friends with an authentic Tuscan meal with what you learn from these cooking lessons here.

If you find that these activities, like the Palio di Siena, and the locales, like the Duomo, are very interesting to you, why not schedule a trip to Siena, Italy today? Call us at 800.955.4418 to find out more about our escorted trips and our customizable trips to Italy.

Siena and Touristic Importance

A fascinating city with a turbulent history of feuds and battles both with its bitter rival, Florence, and indeed within the city itself, much of which remains in evidence today. If you include both Florence and Siena in your itinerary during your holiday in Tuscany you will note - apart from the fact that both Tuscan cities are a modern day feast for the eyes - that the fascination of the two lies in the great contrasts between them. On the simplest level you will immediately note that one is far larger than the other, which in itself is a testimony to how centuries of bitter rivalry shaped them. Most people visit Florence, less include Siena, but if you choose this last city for your stay you will be able to walk its fabulous backstreets and discover that its wonderful history is laid out before you in signs, symbols and many other clues.

There are small ceramic plaques, flags in neighbourhood colours, modern sculptures of different animals interwoven into the city's fountains and, if you are really observant, you will even notice stickers on car bumpers. All of these tell the story of Siena's wealth and position in Medieval Europe, its power struggle with Florence and the internal strife between noble families vying for power. Siena's street signs provide a fascinating insight into its Medieval character, not least because many signs remain to the present day. One sign of 1641, for example, informs prostitutes that the "Most Serene Prince Matthias (the Florentine Governor) forbids them to live on his street" (Via di Salicotto).

In Medieval times Siena, at one point, became the most powerful banking city on the continent. Despite the fractious goings on, the city's nobility managed to organize a strong and sophisticated republic, but the trouble and rivalry, both internal and with its greatest rival Florence, was never far away. Siena continued to be divided into its ganglands, known as contrada and, whilst today these emblems of neighbourhood are more like team colours played out twice a year as a feast for the senses at the city's two palios, in past centuries the families lived in their palazzi building defensive strongholds within the city itself. Sometimes the citizens were so afraid of certain noblemen that roads were built parallel to their palazzi so that they didn't have to walk past them. Before the format of today's Palio, Siena's most popular civic sport was the Gioco del Pugno, essentially an incredible three hundred a side fist fight in the Campo between rival neighbourhoods... When tempers flared, it was not unknown for the axes and crossbows to appear! But whilst noble families certainly fought between themselves, they also united under the flag of the Sienese Ghibellines and spent centuries fighting Florence's Guelph's in a bitter rivalry over power, wealth, influence and territory. Perhaps it was the city's internal conflict and lack of cohesion that eventually led to the territorial and political balance of power swaying in favour of the Florentines.

Siena's finest hour may be recorded in 1260 when Florence had the arrogance to send a herald to the city to demand that its walls be demolished and Siena's large population of "Ghibelline" exiles be handed over... With 40,000 soldiers outside the walls, waiting for the word to raze the city to the ground, Siena, faced with overwhelming odds, dedicated the keys of the city to the Virgin Mary on the altar of the as yet unfinished cathedral. The next morning the Sienese soldiers marched out to the battle of Montaperti to inflict a defeat upon Florence so complete that had they continued on and razed Florence, today's Tuscany might look very different.

However, history records that within a few years the balance of power had swung back to Florence, where it would remain for the next three centuries. The good news for all of us is that by the time Siena's power had really dwindled, in the 14th century, her greatest artistic achievement was almost complete – Siena herself. And if you decide to explore Siena's countryside, those are the views:

Montalcino, Siena Travel Guide

Introduction

Montalcino is a charming hill town near Siena that is mostly known for its locally-produced wine, the Brunello di Montalcino. Its high elevation offers visitors stunning panoramas of the surrounding valleys, as well as that of the lovely orchards and vineyards directly below.

This picturesque town has a long history which dates as far back as the Etruscan era. The first mention of it appears in documents from 814 AD which suggest that a church from the 9th century was already in place by the time that the documents were written. It is suggested that this church was built by the monks from the nearby Sant'Antimo Abbey, and that in the 10th century, the local population spiked as the people from the nearby town of Roselle were fled and settled in Montalcino. During the medieval era, Montalcino was known for its tanneries and leatherworking, and the town's artisans produced high-quality leather items.

Despite being known nowadays as a quiet getaway in the countryside, Montalcino was actually once an independent commune and an important location for trade because of its favorable position along the Via Francigena which served as the main thoroughfare between Rome and France at the time. Over the years, however, it came under the control of the larger city of Siena and it was eventually considered as more of a satellite town.

While Montalcino enjoyed the benefits that a prosperous city such as Siena could offer to its allies, this also meant that they would become involved in any confrontation that the city may be embroiled in. Of particular note would be the tensions between Siena and Florence in the 14th and 15th centuries which plunged Montalcino directly into the fray, up until Florence's powerful Medici family finally conquered Siena in 1555. It is said that despite the fact that Siena has already fallen under Medici rule, Montalcino resisted for another four years before finally succumbing to the pressure.

Nowadays, the citizens of Montalcino celebrate that age by holding a festival twice a year where participants dress up in Medieval costumes, and each of the city's four quarters or contrade, are represented by their respective lords and ladies. These "nobles" then oversee an archery contest and each the people of each contrade cheers for their representatives.

What to See

Wines
If you're going to be in Montalcino, make sure to at least be able to try their world-famous wine, or at least go on a wine tour! The Brunello di Montalcino is made from the locally-grown sangiovese grosso grapes, and is known for being the first type of wine to be granted the appellation Denominazione di Origine Controllata e Garantita (or DOCG) by the Italian government, which is basically a seal of approval and a guarantee that the product was produced on site, and that it was done so according to the highest standards. Brunello di Montalcino wine must be aged five years before it can be sold, while its Riserva version requires at least six years.

Other than the Brunello, there's also the Rosso di Montalcino (DOC) which is aged for one year, the various "Super Tuscan" which are equally wonderful, and the Moscadello sweet white wines.

The Fortress

Montalcino is primarily a medieval town, and as such, is actually a fortified location and is surrounded by walls. These 13th century medieval fortifications remain prominent sights to this day, and visitors can still walk along some of its ramparts. The fortress itself is built at the highest point within the town in order for guards to have the best view possible of the surrounding areas. It was designed by some of Siena's best architects of the time, Domenico di Feo and Mino Foresi, who laid everything out in a pentagonal shape while also incorporating existing structures such as the San Giovanni tower, the keep of Santo Martini, as well as an ancient basilica that soon served as the fortress chapel. The Fortress' claim to fame would be that though Montalcino was conquered at several points, the fortress itself has never fallen, and the invading forces have never been able to claim it.

Musei Riuniti

Montalcino's local civic and diocesan museum, this institution currently occupies a building that used to be a convent several centuries ago. Its collection includes many pieces of art from Sienese artists of the 15th century onwards. There are beautiful wooden and terracotta sculptures as well as paintings and other artwork. The museum also sometimes holds exhibits that feature contemporary art, so be sure to check its schedule to see if there are any special programs on the day of your visit.

Chiesa di Sant'Agostino

Right beside the Musei Riuniti is the 13th century Church of Sant'Agostino with its simple façade that is done in the Gothic-Romanesque style. It has lovely rose windows and is known for its 14th century frescoes within that were created by Sienese artists. Many of the frescoes depict various religious scenes from the life of Christ, including the Scourging of Christ, as well as scenes from the Passion of Christ.

Duomo di Montalcino

Originally built around the year 1000, what was once a simple church dedicated to San Salvatore achieved cathedral status during the 14th century and thus became Montalcino's main place of worship. Unfortunately, the façade that it now has is completely different from the one it had when it was first built, mostly due to extensive renovation during the 19th century, which resulted in a more neo-classical look.

Within the Duomo can be found various works of art, most notable of which would be the *Immaculate Conception with Jesus and God the Father* and *Saint John the Baptist in the Desert* painted by Francesco Vanni of Siena. There are also paintings by Francesco Nasini, as well as reassembled fragments of an 11th century sculpture depicting Christ and two angels.

Palazzo Comunale

Located at the Piazza della Principessa Margherita, the Palazzo Comunale is the primary building in the area. What currently serves as the town hall is a 13th century structure once known as the Palazzo dei Priori. This palazzo proudly displays the coats of arms of the Podesta family who once governed Montalcino. The palazzo comes with a tall medieval tower, while nearby can also be found the arched building called La Loggia which dates back to the Renaissance era.

Other Sights

- Sant'Antimo Abbey
- Badia Ardenga
- Pieve dei Santi Biagio e Donato
- Pieve dei Santi Filippo e Giacomo
- Chiesa di San Michele
- Convento dell'Osservanza
- Chiesa dei Bianchi
- Chiesa del Corpus Domini
- Chiesa della Madonna del Soccorso
- Chiesa di San Francesco
- Chiesa di San Lorenzo in San Pietro
- Chiesa di Sant'Agostino
- Chiesa di Sant'Antonio abate
- Chiesa di Sant'Egidio
- Chiesa di Santa Croce
- Chiesa di Santa Maria delle Grazie
- Former Hospital of Santa Maria della Croce

- ➢ Parish of St. Sigismund in Poggio alle Mura
- ➢ Church of Our Lady of Mercy
- ➢ Parish of St. Michael the Archangel
- ➢ Pieve Santa Restituta
- ➢ Santa Maria Maddalena in Torrenieri
- ➢ Oratory of the Company of San Rocco

Tips and Advice

If you want to take amazing panoramic photos of the area, one of the best places to do so would be up the fortress battlements.

Take it slow. Montalcino is a peaceful, quiet town, so there's no point of trying to rush everything when you're there. Match your pace with your surroundings, and just take the time to enjoy yourself and appreciate the fresh air. As such, make sure you make room in your itinerary for long, relaxing strolls down the city's streets.

When venturing beyond the walls and into the many orchards and vineyards nearby, make sure to wear comfortable footwear, and bring a good map or GPS with you.

If you're looking for wineries to visit, there are many guided wine tours available. However, there are also wineries who don't even have a sign and you will have to walk up to it, and ask for yourself if you can visit, tour the premises, and/or sample their wares.

If you happen to find one of these places, be aware that these are normally family-run establishments that are not equipped for regularly receiving tourists, and the people you encounter here are most likely very busy with their chores and with taking care of their crops. Because of this, don't be surprised if they refuse to receive you, particularly during the autumn season when everyone is expected to help with the harvest. On the other hand, if they agree to entertain you and you set an appointment, make sure to keep that appointment, and once you're there, to be respectful. Remember that they are making time for you despite the demands of maintaining their crops, so be appreciative of that

Monteriggioni, Siena Travel Guide
Introduction

A classic walled medieval town, Monteriggioni is located in between Siena and ColleValdelsa, with its ramparts, winding roads, and soaring towers. It sits atop a natural hill and was built by the Senesis in the 1200s to overlook Cassia Road, a position which allowed it to have control over the Elsa and Staggia Valleys at the time, which made the city rather powerful during the medieval years. It is also one of the best-preserved towns from that era, and many of the streets and structures that we can now find within it are all the original structures. This is what makes it a tourist favorite as walking inside this walled city allows visitors to be transported back in time as they walk in the same streets that people such as Dante Alighieri may have also walked upon.

Monteriggioni boasts of an intact fortified wall, parts of which have been made accessible to the public once more. The view from here is unobstructed, and allows one to gaze upon breathtaking panoramas of the area. It also illustrates as to how this small town was strategically important during the time when Florence and Siena were both fighting over territory as both cities began to expand. It resisted the Florentine attacks for centuries and would have probably done so for much longer, except that in 1554, the man who was entrusted with the garrison, the exiled Florentine Giovannino Zeti, simply handed the literal and figurative keys to the city to the incoming Medici forces as a way to reconcile with his former home city – an act that many locals still consider as an act of great betrayal to this day.

These days, Monteriggioni is a peaceful place that mostly focuses on wine production and tourism, and the local government has stepped up its preservation efforts.

What to See

Piazza Roma
Monteriggioni's main piazza is known as the Piazza Roma. This public space is dominated by a Romanesque church with a simple façade, the Church of Santa Maria Assunta, while the piazza's perimeter is lined by houses in the Renaissance style. These houses were places where the city's nobles, merchants, and gentry once lived. From the piazza, one can also easily access the public gardens which during times of war centuries ago was an important feature of the city. This was because the produce that was once grown here was what provided much-needed sustenance to the citizens during times when their

supply lines may have been cut off by invading forces, thus allowing them to withstand sieges for long periods of time.

Medieval Gates and Towers
Part of Monteriggioni's defensive structures would be the two great gates, namely the Porta Florentina and the Porta Romana. One gate faces Florence to the north, while the other faces Rome to the south. The perimeter wall is also dotted by 14 towers which are set apart at equal distances. It was these towers which allowed the locals to defend their city so well many centuries ago, and it was also a feature than tended to intimidate would-be attackers.

Monteriggioni di Torri si Corona Medieval Festival
If you're ever visiting Monteriggioni, do your best to drop by when this colorful festival is taking place. The Monteriggioni di Torri si Corona (Monteriggioni Crowned by Towers) takes its name from a phrase that the famous poet Dante Alighieri used to describe the city in his masterpiece, The Divine Comedy. In the Dante's words, the city is described:

As with circling roundOf turrets, Monteriggioni crowns his walls;E'en thus the shore, encompassing the abyss,Was turreted with giants, half their lengthUprearing, horrible, whom

Jove from heavenYet threatens, when his muttering thunder rolls.– Dante Alighieri, Hell, canto XXXI, lines 40-45"

Considered as one of the most beautiful festivals in the region, the fair takes place every year in July over two long weekends. During this time, visitors are treated with a chance to go back in time as the city goes into reenactments of its glory days during the medieval ages. There will be people dressed up in medieval costumes and walking around the city as nobles, merchants, knights, minstrels, dancers, and various other types of people you may have met in that age. There will be food and drinks that were common to the period that are available for purchase at the city's castle, and to be able to help yourself to these treats, you will have to exchange your modern day cash to medieval coins. There will also be musical and theatrical performances, activities and entertainment for children, duels, and storytellers.

Abbadia Isola

When visiting Monteriggioni, it would also do well to visit the nearby Abbadia Isola, or Abbey Island. Once surrounded by water, its main structure was the abbey of San Salvatore all'Isola. The abbey is well-known for having provided board and lodging for travelers and pilgrims who were making their way to Rome. These days, it is possible to contact the monks who still reside at the abbey, and if there are rooms available, visitors may arrange to stay a few nights at this peaceful location.

One of the main structures to see here would be the church. It is decorated in the Romanesque style, and houses many important pieces of artwork, including a polyptych above the main altar that was painted by the Sienese artist Sano di Pietro.

Tips and Advice

There is a tourist office that can be found right at Piazza Roma if you require information or assistance.

The easiest way to reach Monteriggioni is by taking the bus from nearby cities such as Florence, Pisa, Siena, and Volterra. There are buses that leave for Monteriggioni at regular intervals, but when making plans to visit, make sure to factor in delays as more often than not, these buses may depart late.

It is also very easy to drive to Monteriggioni, but be aware that you cannot take your vehicle inside the town itself as its streets are very narrow. Instead, there is a parking lot on one of the sides of the hill where everyone is expected to leave their cars at.

The town is small and very easy to explore on foot. However, since no vehicles are allowed, make sure to wear comfortable shoes if you plan to really explore its many streets where many hidden gems can be found.

Palio di Siena Travel Guide

Introduction
Other than its historical buildings, part of Siena's cultural identity would be the Palio, an annual four-day horse racing event which causes life in Siena to pause every July 2 and August 16 as residents celebrate and enjoy the race itself as well as the various events and amusements that accompany it. The first race, the Palio di Provenzano is held on July 2 in honor of the Madonna of Povenzano and her church in Siena. Meanwhile, the second race August 16 each year is the Palio dell'Assunta that is held in honor of the Assumption of Mary.

One can trace the roots of the races to the Medieval ages, when the town's main piazza was the site for a lot of major local events, including public sporting events. At the time, the included events consisted mostly of martial sports such as the pugna (basically a large brawl), jousting, and bull fights. The horse races weren't really introduced until about the 14th century when it was known as the "palli alla lunga" and the race was run across the entire city instead of just within the piazza.

Initially, only one race a year was held on July 2, and it wasn't until much later in 1701, was a second race in August added, and only intermittently. Also, the second palio of the year was originally organized and funded by the winning city ward (or "contrada") from July, and only if they could afford it. This is the reason why the existence of the second race would go on and off over many years. Eventually, the city took over the duties of organizing and funding the second race, and it became an annual event ever since.

Pre-Palio Events
In preparation for the Palio, the city imports truckloads of turf and dirt and lays it all down on the perimeter of the pavement of the main piazza in order to create the race track for the horses. Take note that the piazza is in the shape of a shell, which makes for some very tricky turns. This is why soft protective crash barriers against walls of nearby buildings are also put in place as it is not uncommon for riders to collide into

awkward corners. Designated areas for officials and audiences are also put into place.

In the meantime, while the race grounds are being set up, the fun starts well before either race, when citizens of the seventeen contrade challenge each other. This challenge comes in the form of bands walking through "enemy" neighborhoods in the middle of the night and making the Palio an unholy racket. Eventually, ten neighborhoods earn the right to produce a horse and rider for the day of the race. Not all seventeen contrade can take part in the Palio, but the seven contrade who didn't make it to the races, are automatically included in the next. Meanwhile, the remaining three slots are awarded by lottery which happens during the last week of May and the first week of July.

Horses that will be entered into Palio are picked well in advance of the occasion, and are often the pride of the stables of their respective owners. These horses go through several trial races and veterinary examinations, and three days before the race, the contrade's Capitani (or main representative) then proceeds to select ten horses of equal quality among the many that may be offered to him. Another lottery then determines which of the ten selected horses will represent the contrada at the races. The chosen horse then goes through another six trial races on the evening of the horse selection and again on morning of the day right before before the Palio. The passionate residents of each contrada (the contradaioli) then pray to their patron saint to bless their chosen horse and jockey and help them win the races.

Once the horses and their riders have been selected, the Palio is then kicked off with a mass at the Duomo for the jockeys who are dressed in the traditional manners and wearing their contrade's colors. Next, there is a benediction ceremony for the horses, and it is then followed by a grand parade known as the Corteo Storico that involves around 600 people in full historical costumes.

The Corteo Storico
The Corteo Storico precedes the races itself, and this pageant is nothing short of spectacular. It involves , among many others, the Alfieri, or flag wavers. The Alfieri are dressed in traditional costumes and carry flags that bear the colors and coats of arms of the participating contrade. They then perform dances and acrobatic stunts to the sound of drumbeats, using the waving and tossing of flags to enhance their already-energetic

performance. The whirling colors of the flags, the Alfieri's costumes, and the rhythm of the drums makes for an exciting show that gets the crowd into a festive mood.

There is also a squad of carabinieri on horseback who are dressed in traditional costume, complete with swords and military decorations. The squad then rides their horses down the track, taking one lap at a walk while in formation. After that lap, the next part is a demonstration of a mounted charge and has them riding at full gallop, before exiting down one of the nearby streets and out of the piazza – a quick taste of the main event to further excite the audience.

By 7:30 p.m. for the July race, and 7 p.m. for the August race, an explosive charge is detonated causing a loud sound to echo all across the piazza. This is the signal to the thousands present that the races are about to begin.

Il Palio
At the start of the race, nine jockeys ride their horses bareback into the piazza and to the starting line which is an area in the middle of two ropes. The first nine riders enter the piazza in an order that is determined by lottery. The tenth rider, known as the rincorsa, waits outside as the others make their entrance.

Once the rincorsa finally joins the others between the two ropes, the race starter (called "mossiere") then activates a switch which causes the rope in front of the riders to drop to the ground, and thus releasing rider and horse onto the track.

The race itself runs for three laps and normally lasts for only about 90 seconds or so. However, those 90 seconds are completely action-packed as the piazza's turns and corners can be difficult to maneuver. As a result, it is fairly common for jockeys to get thrown off their horses as everyone gallops to the finish line. A dismounted rider doesn't mean the end for the contrada it represents, though, as a riderless horse can still win the race in a condition known as cavallo scosso.

On top of the hazards of the race track itself, the jockeys are also allowed to make use of whips, not just to spur their own horses forward, but to also disturb their competitors' horses or even take a swat at the other jockeys themselves. Almost everything is allowed at the race track, including pulling or shoving fellow jockeys, or attempting to hamper other horses right at the starting line (to anyone who has ever played the video game *Mario Kart*... you'd probably have a good idea of how this all looks).

The loser in the race is considered to be the contrada whose horse came second, not last.

Once a winning horse has been determined and announced, the Capitani of the winning contrada receives an award in the form of a banner of hand-painted silk that is created by a different artist for every race (this banner is known as a "palio") on behalf of his entire contrada.

Post-Palio Events
The celebrations and festivities don't end at the finish line, however, as the members of each contrada are VERY, VERY passionate about the races that they may continue to celebrate and enjoy their victory up until the next Palio. It is known for contrade who are historical rivals to celebrate the fact that their bitter enemies didn't win, either.

<u>Tips and Advice</u>

The Palio is a major event for the citizens of Siena and is also quite a spectacle that draws in both local and international crowds. Because of this, you might want to arrive very early in the morning of the races if you want to get a good view as the piazza will fill up VERY fast.

Seats can range from plain bleachers to box seats which you can reserve for a fee, but be aware that these tend to get sold out long before the races even begin.

You might also want to book your accommodations well in advance if you plan to stay in Siena throughout the duration of the Palio, as there will be many other visitors who will be around for the races.

Tourists are allowed to join a contrada. Pick one that you like and wear its colors proudly! March with your faction as you heckle and taunt your opponents, and cheer on your contrada's horse and jockey! Be aware, however, that the Sienese are as passionate about the Palio as some people are passionate about soccer or football, so be careful not to hurt anyone's sports pride!

Piazza del Campo, Siena Travel Guide

Introduction

The Piazza del Campo is the historic center of Siena and its main public space. It is considered by many as one of Europe's greatest medieval squares and is known for its beautiful architecture which has served as the backdrop for many a beautiful photograph or painting.

The piazza itself is shaped like a shell and is paved in red brick. From here, eleven streets radiate into the rest of the city, which is why many consider it to be the heart of Siena. Other than its postcard-perfect looks, however, the Piazza is also the venue for one of the city's main attractions, the Palio di Siena horse races which are held twice a year.

It wasn't always the lovely piazza that we know it as, though. In fact, the area where it is now located was formerly a medieval marketplace. As with most marketplaces, people from nearby communities and towns would gather and mingle here to trade and exchange news, particularly those from nearby Camollia, Castellare, and San Martino. Over time, these three communities would join together to form the city of Siena, which was then governed by the Council of Nine, or "Consiglio dei Nove." It was the Council who was responsible for much of the development of the area, adding facilities and infrastructures to their new city.

Nowadays, the Piazza remains Siena's social and civic center, and it isn't uncommon to find people having picnics and relaxing on the pavement. It is also one of the city's tourist hotspot as many of Siena's main attractions can be found just at the perimeter of the Piazza, alongside coffee bars and restaurants.

What to See
Torre del Mangia (Mangia Tower) One of the most recognizable landmarks in Siena, the Torre del Mangia stands at a dizzying 102 meters tall. It was built between 1325 and 1348 by the brothers Francesco and Muccio di Rinaldo, and was most likely finished in white travertine by Agostino di Giovanni. Inside the tower can be found a bell that weighs around 6700 kilos, called "Sunto." It was installed in 1666.

The tower's name literally translates to "Tower of Eating," and according to local legend, this name takes after the tower's first owner, the sculptor Giovanni di Balduccio whose nickname was "il mangiaguadagni" mostly because he tended to squander his money on food because he loved eating so much.

Palazzo Comunale (Palazzo Pubblico)

Located at the bottom of the piazza, and at the base of the Torre del Mangia is the 13th century structure known as the Palazzo Comunale. It was built to be the piazza's centerpiece and is regarded by many as "one of the most graceful Gothic buildings" in Italy. It also serves as home to the Museo Civico.

Fonte Gaia (Gaia Fountain)

According to local historians, it took eight years of backbreaking labor before water was finally routed to the Piazza del Campo in 1342. There was much celebration over this achievement, and to commemorate the event, the "Joyful Fountain" was constructed.

The original fountain was replaced in 1419 by one created by the Renaissance sculptor Jacopo della Quercia, and this version is regarded as an important work of art from that era that was representative of both the Gothic and the Renaissance styles. His fountain sculpture was also considered ahead of his time as it included nude female figures in a public space that did not represent either Eve or a repentant saint.

Unfortunately, this fountain was also removed in the 1800s and replaced by a copy made by Tito Sarrocchi which excluded the female nudes found in della Quercia's version as the Council at the time found it to be too indecent to be put on display in a piazza. Don't worry, however, as della Quercia's work, though severely weathered, is kept safe at the nearby Santa Maria della Scala museum where it can continue to be viewed by the public.

Other Points of Interest

- Cappella di Piazza
- Palazzo Chigi-Zondadari
- Palazzo Sansedoni
- Loggia della Mercanzia
- Casa De Metz
- Costarella dei Barbieri
- Palazzo d'Elci

Tips and Advice

It is possible to climb to the top of the Torre del Mangio. However, be aware that it will be a steep trek to the top as the tower has about 500 steps or so. Wear comfortable shoes if you plan to climb the tower. It will be all worth it, however, as at the top can be seen a breathtaking panorama of the city.

For safety reasons, only 30 people are allowed to be in the tower at any one time, so if you don't want to wait too long for your turn to climb the tower, it may be a good idea to visit during the low season.

Admission to the Palazzo Comunale's ground level central courtyard is free.

Piccolomini Library, Siena Travel Guide

Introduction

For many people who visit the city of Siena, one of the main stops is the Duomo where one can admire the exterior and interior of this beautiful church along with its related areas such as the baptistery. However, one of the things that you cannot afford to miss while at this location would be the gorgeous Piccolomini Library. The library is named after one of the most powerful and prominent families in Siena's history, and in particular, its most well-known member, Enea Silvio Piccolomini.

Enea is first known to have been the mediator during the talks to reconcile the Papal State with Emperor Frederick III, as well as for being the one to arrange the same emperor's marriage with Eleonora of Aragon, as well as his coronation in Rome. These achievements made him rather popular, and as a reward for successfully completing these tasks, he was appointed as the Bishop of Trieste in 1447, and three years later, he was reappointed as the Bishop of Siena. Eventually, in 1456, he became a cardinal until finally in 1458, he was elected pope and took on the name Pius II.

Due to his influence and popularity, it was inevitable that the Piccolomini name took on even more weight in Siena, and this is also the reason why their family crest of the half-moon on a blue background can be seen in many places in the city.

As for the library itself, it was actually established by Enea's nephew, Francesco Todeschini Piccolomini, who himself also became a cardinal as well as the pope whom we know as Pope Pius III. Francesco had the library built in memory of his uncle as well as to house the collection of books and beautifully-illuminated manuscripts that Enea collected throughout his life.

Other than the books and manuscripts, though, it's the library itself that is the real treasure here, as it is quite literally decorated from floor to ceiling. The floor tiles themselves display the family crest, the walls prominently display a series of frescoes, there are lovely sculptures all around, and if you look up, the ceiling itself is a wonder to behold, so make sure to spare enough time to thoroughly enjoy this magical place.

What to See
Frescoes by Pinturicchio

When the library was built, one of the most important artists of the time, Pinturicchio (whose workshop at the time included a young Raphael), was commissioned to decorate it with frescoes. It is said that it was stipulated in his contract that he must produce a series of ten frescoes in his "grotesque" style that would depict the achievements of Enea Silvio Piccolomini, and that he alone must work on it from start to finish without any assistance from his students or assistants. This means that it was Pinturicchio's hand that drew the initial outlines and drafts, and it was also him who painted every single detail in each of the ten massive frescoes.

The frescoes, which were completed in 1508, show the following highlights from Enea's life:

- Enea Piccolomini Leaves for the Council of Basel
- Enea Piccolomini as an Ambassador to the Court of James I of Scotland
- Frederick III Crowning Enea Silvio Piccolomini with a Laurel Wreath
- Homage to Pope Eugenius IV in the Name of Emperor Frederick III

- Enea Silvio Piccolomini Presents Frederick III to Eleonora of Portugal
- Enea Silvio is Elevated to Cardinal
- Coronation of Enea Silvio Piccolomini as Pope Pius II
- Pope Pius II at the Congress of Mantua
- Canonization of Catherine of Siena by Pope Pius II
- Pope Pius II Arrives in Ancona to begin the Crusade

As one looks closely at the frescoes, it couldn't be helped to admire the sheer amount of work that went into every one of them, from the rich colors and rich amount of detail on each figure in the scene, to the beautiful backgrounds, landscapes, and scenery that provide the setting for the characters. If one pays enough attention, you can even spot the Piccolomini family crests in the paintings… along with various self-portraits of the artist and Raphael.

The ten frescoes are separated by painted pillars, and framed by arches that are made to look like red and white marble. These were artistic decisions that were made in order to give the impression that one is looking through a doorway to witness the scene being depicted in the fresco.

Other than to honor the Piccolomini family and Enea Piccolomini, the library was also built in order to house Enea's collection of illuminated manuscripts, along with other illuminated books and documents belonging to Tedeschini (Pius III) and his brother Giacomo which they included in the collection. These exquisite books can be found in protective cases right below the frescoes.

The most important pages on display were those illustrated by some of the most famous artists of the time, including Girolamo da Cremona and Liberale da Verona.

The Three Graces
Prominently displayed in the middle of the room is a statue which shows the three Graces from Roman mythology. The statue itself is an ancient Roman copy of another statue from the Hellenistic period. It was purchased by Francesco Tedeschini from Cardinal Prospero Colonna in Rome.

At some point in the 19th century, this statue was actually removed from the premises because the pope at the time, Pius IX, remarked that it was improper for statues showing the nude female figure to be in what he incorrectly identified as the sacristy of the Duomo. Fortunately, it was returned to its spot later on thanks to a Russian artist who brought it to the attention of then Prince of Naples Vittorio Emanuele, and in 1972, it was made a permanent fixture of the library.

The Expulsion from Paradise
Above the main door of the library is a shrine which depicts Adam and Eve being expelled from Paradise. It is actually a copy of one of the marble panels from the Fonte Gaia by Jacopo della Quercia, but what makes it unique is the inscription below it which were Enea's dying words: *"deum maximum et posteros of / fendi utriusque debeo neuter mihi"* (in Italian, *"Offesi Iddio Massimo e i posteri. A entrambi sono debitore, nessuno di loro a me"*).

The Ceiling
The library's ceiling is nothing short of magnificent. It is painted in blue, red, and gold, and is decorated in the "grotesque" style of painting. At the center of it is the Piccolomini family coat of arms surrounded by paintings depicting various subjects that range from allegorical figures and pastoral life. Two large panels also feature scenes from myths, particularly the Rape of Persephone, and the story of Diana and Endymion.

Tips and Advice

When buying tickets to see the library, try calling the OPA hotline. Multilingual operators are available to assist you with your booking. Make sure to book at least a day in advance.

Opening hours are:

- ➢ March 1 to November 2 – 10:30 am to 7 pm
- ➢ November 3 to February 28 – 10:30 am to 5:30 pm
- ➢ December 26 to January 6 – 10:30 am to 7 pm

There are special opening hours on holy days such as Christmas and other church holidays, as well as during the Palio.

Santa Maria della Scala Travel Guide

Introduction

Santa Maria della Scala (also known as the Hospital, Ospedale, and Spedale) is located in Siena, and as the name suggests was formerly a hospital that was founded in the year 898 by a cobbler named Sorore. It was dedicated to caring for abandoned children, the poor, the sick, and pilgrims of the time, and was funded by bequests and donations from the wealthy and prominent citizens of Siena, as well as by the hospitals own agricultural operations on the land that surrounds it. It was one of Europe's first and oldest hospitals before it was transformed into a museum. After the transformation, it has been credited for having played a major cultural role in the growth of art and culture in Siena.

Located across Siena's Piazza del Duomo, Santa Maria della Scala is actually a complex of buildings. The notable sections include the 13th century Church of the Santissima Annuziata, and the Pellegrinaio or "Pilgrim'sHall" where pilgrims were lodged on their way to other cities such as Florence, Rome, or the Vatican. The hospital is also said to have acquired relics such as a nail from the cross of Christ, the Virgin Mary's girdle and veil, as well as relics from St. Augustinus and St. Marcellinus, all of which may have contributed to the hospital being a popular stop for pilgrims at the time.

In the 1300s, Santa Maria della Scala commissioned many very important interior and exterior frescoes to decorate the premises, along with several significant altar pieces. Unfortunately, the exterior frescoes of the Ospedale no longer exist which is a shame as they were created by important Sienese artists such as Simone Martini and the Lorenzetti brothers, Pietro and Ambrogio. According to records, the frescoes depicted the life of the Virgin Mary and were as follows:

- Santa Maria della Scala currently houses a series of frescoes that Birth of the Virgin by Pietro Lorenzetti
- Purification of the Virgin (often confused with the Presentation in the Temple) by Ambrogio Lorenzetti
- Betrothal of the Virgin by Simone Martini
- Return of the Virgin to her Parents' House also by Martini.

What is unique about these frescoes is that it not only honors Mary, but her parents Saints Joachim and Anne as well. These were the subjects of special devotion at the Hospital during the 1320s and 1330s.

siena-italy-travel-guide-santa-maria-della-scala-Cappella_della_MadonnaThankfully however, the interior artwork of have managed to survived over the centuries, and the artists involved are the likes of Bartolommeo Bulgarini whose altar pieces which housed various relics are of particular note.

By the 18th century, the hospital became part of a university, and in 1995, it was officially opened to the public as a museum. As the years went by, more and more sections of the former hospital was restored and opened for viewing, and until now, renovation and restoration works are ongoing for other still-closed locations.

What to See

Altarpieces
To match the subject of the exterior frescoes that the hospital commissioned, the altarpieces inside the Santa Maria della Scala also depicted scenes from the life of the Virgin Mary. The main painter of these altarpieces was Bartolommeo Bulgarini who was awarded the commission for five of the main altarpieces. Other altarpieces were created by other Sienese artists.

The largest and most extravagant piece that can be found would be that of the Assumption of the Virgin Thi by Bulgarini which, besides being detailed and richly-colored, also makes use of gold leaf. It is particularly ornate as it was meant to serve as a reliquary for the Virgin's girdle which the hospital obtained in the mid-1300s. Another important altarpiece would be the Reliquary Shutters of Andrea Gallerani which was created by an unknown artist. There is also another painting behind the shutters and inside the altarpiece which once again depicts Andrea Gallerani is pictured again.

The Museum
The Museum is composed of several large sections of the complex and span four levels that go down. Three of the levels are open to the public and are organized as follows:

Level 4

- Entrance Hall (Piano terreno)
- Chapel of the Relics/Chapel of the Mantle (Cappella delle Reliquie)
- Palazzo Squarcialupi
- Passeggio
- Lanes East (Corsie est)
- San Leopoldo Hall
- San Giuseppe Hall
- San Pio Hall
- Pilgrim Hall (La sala del Pellegrinaio)

- Sant'Ansano Hall
- Old Sacristy (Sagrestia Vecchia)
- Chapel of the Madonna (Cappella della Madonna)
- Church of the Santissima Annunziata (Chiesa della Santissima Annunziata)
- Young Women's Chapel (Cappella delle Donne)

Level 3

- Hayloft or Barn (Fienile)
- Oratory of the Company of Saint Catherine of the Night (Oratorio di Santa Caterina della Notte)
- Corticella
- Warehouses of the Corticella
- Lanes Center (Corsie centrali)
- The Treasury (Il Tesoro)

Level 1

- National Archeological Museum (Museo archeologico nazionale)

- Company of Saint Mary Under the Vaults (Compagnia di Santa Maria sotto le Volte)
- Chiasso di Sant'Ansano

Museum Ground Floor

Chapel of Women (Cappella delle Donne)

This chapel is the first one that visitors will encounter immediately after leaving the ticketing office. It is the entrance to the complex, and is the side that is closest to the cathedral square. It was built in the mid-1400s as additional lodging to accommodate female pilgrims. There are frescoes and sculptures here that are the works of artists such as Martino di Bartolomeo and Andrea di Bartolo.

Old Sacristy(Sagrestia Vecchia)

This part of the complex was constructed in order to house the precious relics that the hospital purchased in the 1300s. The relics themselves are contained in altarpieces made of materials such as precious metals and stones, and enamels. Meanwhile, its ceiling and walls were painted by Lorenzo Vecchietta , and depict scenes including Christ and the four evangelists and prophets. It is also home to a famous fresco by

Domenico di Bartolo which depicts the Madonna of Mercy, also known as Our Lady of the Mantle which was originally created for the Chapel of the Relics, but was moved here in 1610.

Chapel of the Madonna (Cappella della Madonna)

Accessible from the Old Sacristy, it was built around 1680 and stands at a location of an older chapel dedicated to the Virgin Mary's parents, Saints Joachim and Anna. It houses a set of paintings by Giuseppe Nicola Nasini and his son Apollonio, which consists of two large canvases on one wall, framed by stucco and depicting the Nativity of the Virgin and the Presentation in the Temple. On the opposite wall is a painting which shows the Flight into Egypt. At the altar can also be found another painting by the Sienese painter Paolo di Giovanni Fei which depicts the Madonna and Child being surrounded by seven angels.

Other paintings here show other scenes from Mary's life such as the Coronation of the Virgin Mary, and the Massacre of the Innocents by Matteo di Giovanni.

Church of the Annunciation (Chiesa della Santissima Annunziata)

Located in the oldest part of the complex, it was the original chapel of the hospital and was built in 1257, but was later renovated in the 15th century. Later still, in the 17th century, the main altar was replaced by one made of marble and created by Giuseppe Mazzuoli. Its accompanying altarpiece is a bronze figure of Christ made by Vecchietta Lorenzo. There are also two side altars which were added in the early 18th century.

Atrium

This area leads to the older sections of the hospital complex. The ceiling is decorated in the Renaissance style, and here can also be found many tombstones and burials. There are numerous paintings, frescoes, and sculptures.

Chapel of the Relics/Chapel of the Mantle (Cappella delle Reliquie)

To the right atrium can be found the Chapel of Relics. It was built in the second half of the 14th century in order to house the relics that the hospital purchased in 1359, before the relics were moved to the Old Sacristy many years later. As with other parts of the complex, there are numerous frescoes here which depict various religious figures such as the Virgin Mary, Saint Cosmas and Damian, John the Baptist, and John the Evangelist.

Walkway (Passegio)

The Passegio is a large area which served as the main meeting place at the hospital. This section contains various sculptures and coats of arms of the various families who have helped fund and/or build the hospital, including that of the House of Savoy

Lanes East (Corsie est)

It is a passage that allows access to three larger rooms, the Sala San Pio, St. Joseph Hall, and the Hall San Leopoldo. The Hall of San Pio was mainly used for the treatment of hospital patients and for providing medical assistance, a function that it has performed up until 1975. It has a fresco that depicts two episodes from the life of the Blessed Sienese Giovanni Colombini. It also currently houses a fallery which includes paintings from convents, churches, and oratories of religious orders that were suppressed during the Napoleonic era and the post-unification period. Most of these came from the Palazzo Pubblico, the residence of the Governor of the Medici, as well as Santa Maria della Scalal's own collection of artwork. The St. Joseph Hall hosts a series of plaster casts made by the Sienese sculptor Tito Sarrocchi, and the pieces on display are some of the nearly two hundred plaster models donated by the sculptor to the city of Siena in 1894. The Sala San Leopoldo is currently used to house the museum's permanent collection of art for children.

Pilgrim Hall (La sala del Pellegrinaio)

Possibly the most important section of the entire complex, Pilgrim Hall boasts of its vaulted ceiling that features a series of paintings by many artists from the 14th and 15th centuries. Each fresco is highly detailed and colored exquisitely, which allows visitors to have a glimpse into the lives of the people of that time period. These pieces of art are attributed to Lorenzo Vecchietta, Domenico di Bartolo, Pietro d'Achille Crogi and Giovanni di Raffaele Navesi. This section was originally built to provide lodging for pilgrims who were on their way to Siena or Rome. Over the centuries, it has taken on various roles, including that of being a hospital ward up until 1995.

Lower Floor

Corticella

It is a courtyard that leads to the old barn, the oratory of the Society of Saint Catherine of the Night, the warehouses, and the Treasury.

Barn/Hayloft (Fienile)

Originally used as lodging for travelers and pilgrims, it now houses the original of marbles sculptures of the Fonte Gaia that were creatd by the Renaissance artist Jacopo della Quercia.

Oratorio di Santa Caterina della Notte/Oratory of Saint Catherine of the Night

It is the spot where legend says St. Catherine of Siena was standing in prayer as she comforted and healed the sick. In the seventeenth century, the oratory was enriched by numerous paintings, including four paintings depicting the life of St. Catherine. They were painted by the Sienese painters Rutilio Manetti and Francesco Rustici. Besides the many paintings, carvings, reliquaries and furnishings, the Company also retains a beautiful altarpiece by Taddeo di Bartolo which depicts the Madonna and Child, Four Angels, and Saints John the Baptist and Andrew.

The Treasury (Il Tesoro)

As the name suggests, this is the part of the complex where the hospital's valuables are kept. It housed relics along with their containers made of gold, silver, glass, filigree, and precious stones, a lot of which hail from the imperial chapel of Constantinople. There were also crates of jewelry, chalices, other reliquaries of various shapes, including one due to the famous goldsmith Goro di ser Neroccio. Along with the treasures were important books and documents, as well as illuminated manuscripts with cover plates made of gold with enamel. Among the collection are also altarpieces and silk tapestries with gold thread which feature stories of Christ and the saints.

Lowest Level

National Archaeological Museum of Siena

Since 1993, the complex has served as the home for the National Archaeological Museum of Siena. Set up in the underground rooms that were originally used for as storage and warehouses, now reside the archaeological collections that have been recovered within Siena. The space spans about 2500 square meters.

Company of Saint Mary Under the Vaults (Compagnia di Santa Maria sotto le Volte)

Originally headquartered at the Siena Cathedral, these companies and brotherhoods moved to the complex in the 1700s. The members of the order are known for providing their assistance to the everyday operations of the hospital. In their area can be found a beautiful wooden crucifix between the terracotta figures of Saint Bernardino and Saint Catherine, and on the altar of the oratory is placed a canvas made by depicting the Madonna and Child with Saints Peter and Paul. The sacristy also contains interesting frescoes attributed to Andrea Vanni and Luca di Tommè .

Other Museum Attractions

- Art Museum for Children
- Center of Contemporary Art
- Giuliano Briganti Library and Photo Library of Art
- Additional spaces for temporary displays and international conventions
- Flags from all of the Contrade of Siena

- ➢ Palazzo Squarcialupi

Tips and Advice

The museum is open almost every day of the year, from 10:30 am to 6:30 pm. Admission fee is EUR 10, and reduced rates are available for groups, students, seniors, and soldiers. Residents, children under 11 years old, and disabled persons can enter for free.

In case it hasn't been made apparent yet, the Santa Maria della Scala complex is humongous. Be prepared to spend a whole day or more here, and make sure to wear comfortable footwear.

San Gimignano Travel Guide

Introduction

San Gimignano is a small walled medieval hill town in the province of Siena that is also known by its other name, "The Town of Fine Towers" thanks to the numerous towers that can be found all over town. It is a UNESCO World Heritage Site as it contains some of the finest examples of medieval and renaissance art and architecture. On top of that, San Gimignano is also known for its white wine, the Vernaccia di

San Gimignano, that is produced from the ancient variety of Vernaccia grape grown on its hillsides.

The location that we now know as San Gimignano started out as a small Etruscan village that has been around since 3 BC, and has since survived events such as the Catiline conspiracy against the Roman Republic as well as invasions from Attila the Hun. By the 6th century, a church was built and the village began to grow around it. By the middle ages and during the Renaissance, this flourishing town became a popular stopover for travelers and pilgrims who were making their way to Rome and the Vatican. Its economy also began to grow in earnest due to the local production of wine and saffron which was in high demand.

The towers that the town is most known for didn't appear until the 1300s, however. At the time, many rival families were vying for prestige within the town walls, and as a way to flaunt their power and wealth, each family would build towers at their homes, and the towers just got taller and taller as they attempted to outdo each other. This practice was only stopped when it was ordained by the local government that no tower should be built higher than the Palazzo Comunale. Later on, as the town submitted to the Florentine rule of the Medicis, many of the towers were reduced in height to match that of the houses and give the area a more uniform look.

Since that time, very little has changed in the development and infrastructure of this town, and many of those that visitors can find there are the original buildings. It has been made even more famous in recent years when the entire town was mapped out and accurately reproduced and rendered in a popular video game. In the game, San Gimignano is one of the main locations that players can visit and explore, and those who have walked down its streets and piazzas within the game, tend to become interested in visiting the real location to see for themselves how closely matched the real town and the digital versions are.

What to See

Piazza della Cisterna
The main piazza of San Gimignano, this public space is triangular in shape and is lined with medieval houses and palazzos, some of which are considered to be some of the finest examples of Romanesque and Gothic design. In the middle of the piazza can be found the town's well and main

water source, which is how the piazza got its name. At this piazza can be found the towers of the Ardinghelli family, the tower of the Benuccis, the Casa Rodolfi, Palazzo Razzi, as well as Palazzo dei Cortesi.

Piazza Duomo
To the north of Piazza della Cisterna is the Piazza Duomo where one can find the Collegiata of Santa Maria Assunta that is reachable via a flight of stairs. Other important buildings that can be found here are the Palazzo Comunale and the Palazzo Podesta which serves as the mayor's residence. The majority of public and private monuments can also be found here, including Torre della Rognosa and Torre Chigi, Palazzo del Popolo, as well as Torre Grossa which faces the twin towers of the Salvuccis.

Towers
The town's most distinguishing feature, the towers can be found in various locations. Of the original 72 towers, 14 of varying heights remain intact. These are namely:

- Campanile della Collegiata
- Torri degli Ardinghelli
- Torre dei Becci

- Torre Campatelli
- Torre Chigi
- Torre dei Cugnanesi
- Torre del Diavolo
- Torre Ficherelli or Ficarelli
- Torre Grossa
- Torre di Palazzo Pellari
- Casa-torre Pesciolini
- Torre Pettini
- Torre Rognosa
- Torri dei Salvucci

Palazzo Pubblico/Pinacoteca Civica

Once the main administration building of the town, it is now a prominent gallery which contains important works of art including those by masters such as Filippino Lippi, Pinturicchio, Taddeo di Bartolo, Benozzo Gozzoli, Domenico di Michelino, Memmo di Filippuccio, Pier Francesco Fiorentino, and many more. It mainly features both Florentine and Sienese artists.

Ferie delle Messi and the Giostra dei Bastoni

The Ferie delle Messi is an annual medieval fair that is held on the third weekend of June. During this time, the piazzas and streets of San Gimignano take on the air of a medieval castle as people walk around in costumes representing nobles, knights, merchants, artisans, and performers of the time period. The Knights of Santa Fina hold mounted jousts using lances (the event is known as the Giostra dei Bastoni), and there are plus food and drink stands where one can sample local cuisine and specialties such as olive oil, wine, and saffron.

There is also a large arts and crafts market that comes up, and the air is livened further by street performers, wandering musicians, and minstrels. On Sunday afternoon during the festival, the costumed horsemen and characters are then paraded in the Historical Pageant, and the event is capped off by tournaments at the Parco della Rocca that representatives of the four quarters of San Gimignano participate in. The winning quarter then parades throughout the city and the merrymaking continue well into the night.

Tips and Advice

San Gimignano is a popular destination and hence, is normally packed with tourists. When visiting, especially during the summer, brace yourself for a formidable crowd. If you wish to get some breathing space, try visiting either during the low seasons, or if it can't be helped, during early mornings (best if you're staying within the town itself), late afternoons when most of the daytrippers have left, or evenings when other tourists have returned to their hotels.

Make sure to try the local wine, the Vernaccia di San Gimignano. It is a white wine and goes well with seafood, and is also good as an aperitif. Many shops offer free wine tastings, so grab a bottle if it catches your fancy. However, be prepared to pay for good quality wine.

San Gimignano is a very small town and can be easily explored on foot. If arriving by car or bus, you must leave your vehicle outside the city walls.

There is a shuttle bus within the town that operates for the entire day, and can take visitors from one of the main gates, Porta San Giovanni, to Piazza della Cisterna, to the other gate on the other side of town, Porta San Matteo. Bus tickets only cost a few euros and can be bought at the Tourist Information office or at any tobacconist's shop (tabacchi).

The Collegiata is worth a visit for its frescoes depicting scenes from the Old and New Testaments of the Bible. Admission fee is EUR €3.50, and combo tickets are also available. Its opening hours are Mondays to Fridays from 9:30 am to 7:30 pm, Saturdays from 9:30 am to 5:00 pm, and Sundays from 12:30pm to 5:30 pm.

The admission fee for the Pinacoteca Civica in the Palazzo Pubblico is EUR 5. The ticket price includes Torre Grossa. Audio guides are available for EUR 2. From March to October, it is open daily from 9:30 am to 7:00 pm, while from November to February, its hours are from 10:00 am to 5:00 pm.

The Church of Sant'Agostino contains frescoes which depict the life of St. Augustine painted by Benozzo Gozzoli. You can approach the friendly, English-speaking friars at the premises who can provide you with more information about the church. Masses are still held here, and English mass is held on Sundays at 11:00 am. The church is open daily from 7:00 am to 12:00 pm, and again at 3:00 pm to 7:00 pm. Admission is free, but be sure to keep some change in your pocket as the church makes use of coin-operated lighting boxes. To illuminate a painting for better viewing, you will need to use a EUR 0.50 coin. The light will remain on for a few minutes before you will need to drop another coin in.

Every Thursday, there markets pop up at the Piazza della Cisterna and at the Piazza del Duomo.

The Tourist Information center is at the Piazza del Duomo. You can find free maps, room-booking services, bus tickets, as well as a free bag check service here. For a few euros, they also offer audio guides for walking around the town's streets, and from March to October, an English/Italian guided walking tour also starts here at 3:00 pm daily except on Sundays.

Monuments In Siena

Siena, with its uniquely preserved medieval architecture, satisfies every art lover and many others as well. From tiny piazzas shared by you and a couple of pigeons to stately 14th and 15th century buildings, there is always something to notice and admire. Limited traffic within the city centre enhances your experience and adds to the feeling of stepping back in time into a medieval world. The following are a few of the sights that are worth spending time visiting.

At the heart of Siena is the Piazza del Campo, famous for its shell-shape, and still the focus of city life. Within the square in the Fonte Gaia, a fountain unique in its quadrangular form and beautiful figures around the edges. The original by Jacopo della Quercia is now in Santa Maria della Scala, but a copy by Tito Sarrocchi gives an accurate account of this remarkable water feature for the visitors today.

Palazzo Pubblico - Torre Del Mangia
The famous Torre del Mangia and the Palazzo Pubblico form one of the sides of Piazza del Campo. The tower, built in 1848 and 102 metres high, gives excellent views over Siena and the surrounding countryside. Palazzo Pubblico, built between 1297 and 1342 is an example of classic Gothic architecture in Tuscany, and houses an amazing array of frescoes by artists such as Vecchietta, Simone Martini and Sodoma

Duomo Of Siena
The Duomo or cathedral is a beautiful building, a mix of Gothic and Romanesque architecture with dark green and white marble in the facade. It contains works by many artists, including Donatello, Pisano and Arnolfo di Cambio. One of its

main attractions is the marble-inlaid floor, to which many artists contributed. The museum of the Duomo, in the same piazza, contains some original statues by Pisano moved for conservation and many artworks, including the famous "Maesta" by Duccio di Buoninsegna. In the same piazza as the Duomo is the hospital of Santa Maria della Scala, which now houses a museum complex, exhibiting frescoes, works of art, temporary shows and treasures collected during its millenial history.

Visit Siena Cathedral And The Gate Of Heaven.
Don't loose the occasion to see the Gate of Heaven, inside the Siena Cathedral.

The splendid route near the ceiling vaults, will lead you through a suggestive way, where you will enjoy beautiful panorama "inside" and "outside" the Cathedral, admiring art treasures such as the famous pavement, the multicolored windows by Ulisse De Matteis, sculptural monuments. From there you can admire a splendid view of Siena and its monument.

Church Of San Domenico
Inside a fresco by Andrea Vanni representing Saint Catherine is conserved. On the left side of the church a chapel with a wonderful marble altar hosts the head of the saint. The crypt

preserves another fine work, a golden cross painted by Sano di Pietro.

Church Of San Agostino
It hosts many works of art, by Vanni and Manetti. In the 15th-century chapel called the Bichi chapel, there are many frescoes by Martini and Signorelli. The Piccolomini chapel has a fresco by Lorenzetti.

Address: Prato S.Agostino, 1

Phone: 0577 226785 / Fax: 0577 206 794

Piazza Salimbeni
Three important buildings mark the piazza of Salimbeni, but the Palazzo Salimbeni is the most important, marking the headquarters of the Sienese bank Monte dei Paschi di Siena, founded more than 500 years ago. Inside the palace is a rich collection of paintings and works of art, which are possible to see by appointment.

MUSEUMS IN SIENA

Siena's museums are filled with fine examples of paintings and sculpture from the Romanic, Gothic and Pre-Renaissance periods. Aside from museums, the town is filled with Gothic architecture and the art of the Sienese school. You will not want to miss Siena's many small churches, and historical squares either. Here is a list of museums of interest:

Museums In Siena

Accademia dei Fisiocritici Museo di Storia Naturale

The collection includes geological, zoological, anatomical and botanical sections.

Address: Prato S.Agostino, 5 Piazzetta Silvio Gigli 2

Phone/Fax: 0577 47002

Archivio di Stato (Museum of the Biccherna Tablets)

Open only upon request in the mornings (closet Saturday and Sunday). In Palazzo Piccolomini, typical style of Florentine Renaissance, this museum holds the ancient tablets of the state ledgers and a collection of ancient manuscripts and books.

Address: Palazzo Piccolomini, Banchi di Sotto 52

Phone: 0577 247 145 / Fax: 0577 446 75

Ticket: Free

Battistero

Behind the Duomo, this baptistry holds a marble font by Jacopo della Quercia, with bronze panels depicting the life of Saint

John the Baptist (designed by Lorenzo Ghiberti and Donatello amongst others).

Duomo of Siena

Siena's Duomo (Cathedral) and its Libreria Piccolomini (holds frescos which tell the story of the life of Pope Pius II, and elaborately illustrated books). The Duomo also hold precious frescos, sculptures, stained glass designs and marble masterpieces.

Museo dell'Opera del Duomo

Located in the corner where the larger Duomo would have been. Sacred works from 1300 to 1500 are found here, including work by Duccio. In the Galleria della Statua, you will find the sculpture of Giovanni Pisano, titled Jacopo della Quercia a Donatello. There is an outdoor walkway with a panoramic view of Siena, which is not to be missed.

Address: Piazza del Duomo, 8

Phone: 0577 42309 - 283 098 / Fax: 0577 280 626

Museo Civico (Civic Museum)

At Palazzo Pubblico, the Museo Civico holds masterpieces of Sienese art. The astronomical frescos in the Sala del Mappamondo and the Sala della Pace are not to be missed.

Frescos from the 19the century, which depict Italy's first king, can also be found there. You can climb to the top of the bell tower (Torre del Mangia), for a stunning view of Il Campo, Siena and the surrounding countryside.

Address: Palazzo Comunale, Il Campo (Via), 1

Phone: 0577 292 226 / Fax: 0577 292 296

Museo d'Arte per Bambini (Art's museum for kids)

A specific section with activities and programs designed to offer children exposure to art is located inside the monumental complex of Santa Maria della Scala.

Address: Piazza Duomo, 1

Phone: 0577 534511

Museo della Società Esecutori Pie Disposizioni (Museum of the Society of Executors of Charitable Funds)

Open to the public since 1938, this museum contains an interesting collection of works of art from the Sienese school from the 14th - 18th C. Some notable works are La Sacra Famiglia con San Giovannino of Sodoma and Santa Caterina conduce a Roma il Papa of Girolamo of Benvenuto. Working hours: Mon-Fri 9.00-13.00, Tue and Thu 15.00-17.00. For groups reservation is required.

Address: Via Roma 71
Phone: 0577 284 300

Museo Geomineralogico e Zoologico
Geological/Mineralogical/Zoological Museums
Address: Accademia dei Fisiocritici, Prato di S. Agostino 5
Phone/Fax: 0577 47002

Oratorio di S.Bernardino (Oratory of S. Bernardino)
Built during the 1400s, the interiors feature Mannerist frescoes by Domenico Beccafumi. Beautiful wood and wall paintings are found in this baptistry, located near San Francesco Church.
Address: Piazza San Francesco
Phone: 0577 283 048 / Fax: 0577 280 626

Pinacoteca Nazionale (National Picture Gallery)
This museum holds the largest collection of Sienese paintings, including great masters from the 12th century through the first half of the 17th century and works painted on backgrounds of gold leaf. Discover masterpieces by Duccio di Buoninsegna, Simone Martini, Pietro and Ambrogio Lorenzetti and other artists of the Sienese School here.
Address: Palazzo Buonsignori, S. Pietro (via di), 29
Phone: 0577 281 161 - 286 143 / Fax: 0577 270 508

Santuario Di Santa Caterina Da Siena

This popular tourist spot was once the home of Saint Catherine. Inside, you can see the Oratorio della Cucina (built around 1482) which was once the family kitchen, and the Oratorio della Camera where Siena's patron saint once rested.

Address: Costa di S. Antonio/ corner Via Fontebranda

Santa Maria della Scala Complesso museale (Santa Maria della Scala Hospital)

What is now a museum was once of Europe's first hospitals that offered pilgrims hospitality, and extended its care to the poor and homeless. Inside, you will find a fine collection of work by Sienese artists, and a look at life of the "Spedale," depicted in frescoes that decorate the Sala del Pellegrinaio.

Address: Piazza del Duomo, 2

Phone: 0577 224 811 / Fax: 0577 224 829

Sinagoga

Located behind Piazza del Campo, the old Synagouge of Siena can be visited on Sundays.

Address: Via delle Scotte 14

Open only on Sundays.

Parks & Gardens In Siena

Orto Botanico (Botanical Garden)

A splendid natural area in the heart of the city with many plant species.

Address: Via Pier Andrea Mattioli, 4

Phone: 0577 232 871 / 0577.29.88.74 / Fax: 0577 232 860

Opening Times: Monday-Friday 8.00 - 12.30 / 14.30 - 17.30; Saturday: 8.00 - 12.00; closed on Sundays

Ticket Free

The Botanical Garden, Orto Botanico, was founded in 1784 by Biagio Bartalini. The entrance is located by Piazza Sant Agostino. The garden of two and a half hectars lies in a small valley just inside walls located by Porta Tufi of Siena. Various plants are displayed in three different sections of the garden. The first section contains local varieties of plants from Tuscany, including and some examples of herbs used for medicinal, aromatic and culinary purposes. A second section contains aquatic plants, along with more exotic trees and shrubs, unable to withstand the local climate, such as quince, pomegranate and jujube. A third section is dedicated to fruit bearing plants, and plants of the cactus and agavi families. The tepidarium is used to protect plants found in semi-desert regions, such as American cacti and African euphorbia.

The origins of the garden date back to the beginning of the 17th century, when the Orto dei Semplici of the hospital of Santa Maria della Scala was used for the cultivation of plants with medicinal properties. In 1856, the garden was moved to its current location.

La Lizza
This public garden and its fountain are located in front of the Forte di Santa Barbara, a fortress built by Cosimo I of the Medici family after the Florentines conquered Siena. The fortress was opened for public use in 1778. The area inside the Fortress, Piazza della Liberta, is used for recreational activies, festivals, the summer film series. A view of Siena and the surrounding fields can be enjoyed from the height of the bastions of the 16th century fortress. The Fortress is also the home of the Enoteca Italiana, the Italian Wine Cellar, a center for wine. The Enoteca Italiana sponsors exhibitions, events, and conferences on wine all over the world.

Orto De' Pecci
A cooperative garden with a fabulous view of the Torre del Mangia. To reach this cooperative garden, walk to Piazza del

Mercato, then take the stairs leading down to the field of green below. Take the small street which bears to the right of Via Del Sole. A short walk down this road and past the gate, is pleasant and filled with the aroma of lavendar, rosemary and plants of the Tuscan countryside. The view of the Torre del Mangia and of Piazza del Mercato is fabulous from this peaceful spot

Le Fonti Di Siena

In just about every part of Siena, there are le fonti, "fountains" -- big or small, massive or elegant, charming or historical -- to sit by and admire. As Siena had no nearby fresh water source, acquecducts and complex irrigation systems were made in and around the city. Many fountains were built on what was once the outskirts of Siena; these were multi-purpose basins of water, for cooking, drinking and agricultural use, with roofs protecting water from pollution. These fountains became the gateways to the city, and the city's water was highly regarded and protected.

Aside from Siena's most historical fountains or most impressive, such as Fonte Gaia at Piazza Del Campo, each contrada has a fountain which celebrates its symbol for that part of the city, and serves as the site for the outdoor baptisms each year. From the fountain of the contrada del Brucco, with its large caterpillar in the background, to the fountain of Onda, with the dive of a graceful dolphin, Siena's contrada fountains serve as community meeting places. During the Spring and Summer, these fountains are often surrounded by groups of men talking, or children playing and laughing. The fountains of each contrada should be noted, as each one is different, and speaks of the character of that part of Siena.

Fonte Gaia is considered to be "the queen of Sienese fountains" both for for its central position, Piazza del Campo, also as a work of art. At 321 meters above sea level, Fonte Gaia is situated at the highest elevation of all the fountains. It brings water from the northern part of the city, along a ridge uninterrupted by valleys. The panels of the fountain, completed by Jacopo della Quercia between 1409 and 1419, are considered to be fine examples of Italian sculpture for that period. The originals of Jacopo della Quercia can be seen in the loggia of the Palazzo Comunale. Today, "Ci vediamo alla fontana," is often said, and everyone knows that it means the meeting point is in front of the town's most famous and easy to spot fountain.

Cited by Dante in Canto 30 of the Inferno, Fontebranda is the oldest and perhaps most impressive of the Sienese fountains. This fountain is associated with the birth and early life of Saint Catherine, and she is for this reason is known as the Saint of Fontebranda. Today, Fontebranda is a site for outdoor concerts and dance performances during the summer.

Excursions Around Siena

Around Siena the countryside is perfect for all types of slow travel, excursions on foot, horseback or by bicycle that give the body and mind a fresh surge of vitality, away from our daily routine and stress. Footprints, bicycle tracks and hoof marks appear and disappear with the changing of seasons, and these itineraries are an invitation to the discovery of yet another aspect of this wonderful land.

From Siena you can plan some wonderful days or weekends in the country side. Or even just day trips as many places are within an hour and a half's distance from Siena using public transport or some travel agency from Siena

Montepulciano
Montepulciano is a medieval village in the province of Siena. Close to Pienza, it's 70 km far from Siena, the hill town (with an

elevation of 605 m) is famous for the wine (Vino Nobile di Montepulciano) and for the "pici", a traditional dish.

In the village of Montepulciano visit Antonio da Sangallo's San Biagio, a wonderful Renaissance church.

You can then spend time walking the streets and feel what it was like to live in the medieval period.

Pienza
Pienza is a Renaissane town in the heart of Val d'Orcia (province of Siena). It's been completely rebuilt in the mid-15th century (also the name, before it was called "Corsignano") thanks to Enea Silvio Piccolomini (Pope Pius II), turned this out of the way hill town into a testing ground for the most advanced Renaissance ideas about urban planning.

The project was UNESCO declared Pienza a World Heritage Site in 1996 (in 2004 the entire Val d'Orcia was declared World Heritage Site).

Take a mourning to walk the streets before moving onto the next village.

San Gimignano
San Gimignano is a medieval town that owes its famous skyline to the rival families who tried to outdo each other by building

taller and taller towers. Of the original 76 towers only 13 still survive today. It's famous also for its white wine: the Vernaccia di San Gimignano. It' been declared World Heritage Site by UNESCO.

Asciano
This hill town is a medieval oasis upper the Ombrone valley, in the very heart of "Crete" desert. It was founded by Etuscan, then it becames a Roman village and in XIII century it was purchased by the Sienise.

Asciano has many historical monuments, between them the Romanesque Basilica di Sant'Agata within the 15th century ramparts

Bagno Vignoni
Besides being a pleasant little town set up like a terrace on the Orcia valley, it has a thermal water basin right in the middle of the town square. It is a popular spa town with both an official spa and outside stone culverts with thermal water running in the open.

Le Crete
The name comes from the "crests" of clay eroded over the centuries into a dramatic desert of parched hillocks. The area is home to some of the most remote vestiges of the Sienese

heritage in the enchanting scenery of the Val d'Orcia area. This unique natural landscape has inspired countless poets, writers and painters. only 13 still survive today.

Montalcino

South of the "Crete" , this enchanting fortified hill town is well-known for its red Brunello wine.

The city walls were built in the thirteenth century. The fortress was built on the highest point of the city in 1361 and includs the tower of Saint-Martin, the tower of St. John and an old church, that now is the chapel of the castle. A wine cellar (Enoteca) in the castle offers local wines for tasting and purchase.

Monteriggioni

This enchanting little hill town just 15 km north of Siena has an almost intact circular 13th century fortification wall enclosing the village. It used to be part of Siena's defence system against Florentine attacks.

During Summer there's an Opera Festival inside the Monteriggioni Castle, visit our page dedicated to Opera and Classical Concert in Monteriggioni!

Monte Oliveto Maggiore

This 14th century Benedictine monastery stands on a rocky ridge near Asciano in a scenic park of traditional tuscan trees. The nave's choir stalls count among Italy's finest works of inlaid wood carvings.

Sant'antimo
The 12th century Benedictine abbey, 10 km south of Montalcino enjoys a delightful setting amid olive groves.Translucent onyx and alabaster in the bases of the columns give the nave a delicate light.

San Quirico D'orcia
This fortified town 15 km east of Montalcino was a major stop for north european pigrims journeying to Rome in the Middle Ages. The amazing view of the Orcia valley can be enjoyed from Piazza della Libertà.

Travels In Tuscany

From Siena you can plan some wonderful weekends as many places are within an hour and a half's distance from Siena using public transport or some travel agency from Siena. Here a list of suggested place to be seen in Tuscany

Florence

Florence, capital of the region of Tuscany, has a population of around half a million inhabitants, spreads on the banks of the Arno, between the Adriatic and the Tyrrhenian seas, almost in the middle of the Italian peninsula. It is a city which bustles with industry and craft, commerce and culture, art and science. Being on the main national railway lines, it is easily accessible from most important places both in Italy and abroad.

Founded by the Romans in the first century B.C., Florence began its rebirth after the decadence of the barbaric ages, in the Carolingian period, and reached its highest pinnacles of civilization between the 11th and 15th centuries, as a free city, balancing the authority of the Emperors with that of the Popes, overcoming the unfortunate internal dispute between Guelfs and Ghibellines. In the 15th century, it came under the rule of the Medici family, who later became the Grand Dukes of Tuscany. This in fact was the period when the city was at the height of its glory in art and culture, in politics and economic power. The Grand Duchy of the Medicis was succeeded, in the 18th century, by that of the House of Lorraine, when in 1860 Tuscany became part of the Kingdom of Italy of which Florence was the capital from 1865 to 1871. In this century, the city has once more taken up its role as an important centre for culture and the arts.

Lucca

Lucca, is a small city still surrounded by its original defensive walls; one of Europe's finest and most beautiful circuits of defensive walls came to being as Lucca lies near the sea and is protected on three sides by mountains, hence allowing access to Italy's second largest agricultural plain to be controlled.

In the center of town an ancient Roman racetrack has evolved into the main market square, right next to the cathedral. A visit to the Palazzo Ducale, where Maria Luisa of Borbone and Elisa Bonaparte lived (rumors say that Napoleon slept here too) is well worth it.

Arezzo

In AREZZO you will see traces of different civilizations and traditions: the Etruscans, the roman and the medieval. Petrarca, Piero della Francesca, Luca Signorelli, Giorgio Vasari were all born here. In Arezzo you can see Piero della Francesca's famous fresco cycle depicting the Legend of the Cross. These are the frescoes that Juliette Binoche gets to look at while dangling from a rope in the movie "The English Patient."

A visit to this part of the region allows you to discover, besides the artistic, architecture and religious beauty, the little medieval villages located in this area. If you hire a car you can follow the wine route: for about 200 km through various wine growing areas: Chianti DOCG, Chianti Colli Aretini DOCG, Colli Etruria Centrale DOC, Valdichiana DOC and Cortona DOC as well as Vin Santo. You will see vineyards, olive groves, tobacco plantations, chestnut trees and for.

Pisa
During the Roman époque PISA was a prosperous sea- town, however, the barbaric invasion left the city in ruins and only when the citadel became a free town did it acquire, with the passing of time, more political and economical independence. The XI and XII centuries were a time of splendor; in this period, the city had primary importance inside the Italian peninsula and the Mediterranean Sea thanks to its maritime business and the conquering of Sardinia, Corsica, and several Balearic Isles. In the major tourist attraction in Pisa is of course the leaning Tower along with the Baptistery and the Camposanto, all of them built between the XI and the XII century.

Elba Island

Immersed in the crystalline waters of the Tyrrhenian Sea, Elba Island in Italy is the ideal place to spend unforgettable holidays. Rich in history, art and tradition, the Island is a little peace of Paradise for all those who want to live in touch with an unpolluted nature and practice snorkeling, trekking, diving, archaeological walks and many other outdoor sports

Walking & Bike Tours In Siena

Although we admit that the Siena's hills do not make it a town for easy bike riding, it can offer a range of challenging roads and trails, and an opportunity to admire one of Italy's most romantic towns and surrounding countryside, while getting some excercise at the same time. A day of biking in and around Siena can be a once in a lifetime experience -- a day filled with country roads filled with farmhouses, vineyards, cypress trees and landscapes of endless beauty.

You have the option of renting a road bike or mountain bike by the hour, day or week. Also, contact the stores for information about organized bike tours, where they drive you in a van to a site in the countryside, provide helmets, bikes and guided tours, offering an unforgettable day! Scooters can also be rented, for those who want to cruise around Italian style.

Centro Bici - D.F. Bike

Mountain Bike rental service. It also organise trips and bike tours all around Siena.

Address: Strada Massetana Romana 54

Phone/Fax: 0577 271 905

Official guides for walking & bike tours

La strada bianca di Riccardo Giamello

Phone: ++39 057741254 / Mobile: ++39 3296171952

e-mail: robertaguerri@hotmail.com

Britta Ullrich

Phone: ++39 0577377904 / Mobile: ++39 3394695557

e-mail: britta_ullrich@virgilio.it

Itineraries In Siena

The Augustinian hermitages and the Great Duke's tunnel. Ten minutes far from Siena, inside the thick Lake's wood, a plunge into the past life in search of two Augustinian hermitages (monasteries): we'll visit Lecceto's hermitage, a place of great quietness and meditation, the hermits' grottoes, San Leonardo's hermitage, with the wonderful frescoes painted by Lippo Vanni, and, great conclusion, we'll walk through the

Great Duke's tunnel, an incredibile subway digged more than two centuries ago to reclaim the next marshlands of Pian del Lago.

Bagno Vignoni
There's a village in Tuscany where the main square consists of a large rectangular pool with thermal water coming out from the underground at 42 °C of temperature: leaving from this charming place, whose name is Bagno Vignoni, we'll go to visit the older village of Vignoni Alto, Ripa d'Orcia's castle, bravely overlooking Orcia's gorges, we'll go down to the same river at the point of the ruined medieval bridge and, back to Bagno Vignoni, we can let us take a wonderful hot bath at the Spa swimming-pool.

From Montalcino to Sant'Antimo
From Brunello's homeland a nice crossing leading us to Castelnuovo dell'Abate, pretty village with a view on Mount Amiata, the highest peak of Siennese provincia. After the easy crossing of Lume Spento's pass, we'll go down to the small hamlet named Villa a Tolli, going on to the splendid green hollow where stands out Sant'Antimo's abbey, so precious for travertin and onyx, such an important center of spiritual and temporal power in the Middle Ages.

The little known Chianti
A delightful and aerial "chiantigiana" crossing from the eighteenth century San Donato in Perano's villa to Meleto's castle. We'll visit Vertine, an almost untouched fortified hamlet, Spaltenna's Romanesque church, simple and beautiful, and other small little known places. At the end, the tour of Meleto's castle, built in the Middle Ages but restored inside in eighteenth century style, and wine-tasting of the DOC and DOCG there produced.

Castelvecchio di San Gimignano
Do you know San Gimignano's Towers? Yes, of course! Have you ever been in Castelvecchio; an ancient medieval village, object of strife for centuries between San Gimignano and Volterra? I think you haven't! Here's to you the best opportunity to visit this wild and full of history place: a beautiful walking tour in the countryside around S.Gimignano, with the sightseeing of other small villages as San Donato and Montauto.

In the land of the truffle
For some years San Giovanni d'Asso, remote village in the Siennese countryside, has made the headlines for the richness in with truffle that the able local searchers can find through the

claylands surrounding the village. From this spot, in full immersion in the magic world of Siennese Claylands, we'll go to Monteoliveto's abbey, a place of great fascination and beauty. Panoramas crown the tour.

Naturally fine
Farma's creek: from Petriolo to Iesa we'll go up the most charming watercourse of Siena's provincia, wrapped up in a lush vegetation, and we can take a bath in the fantastic natural pools along the creek. It's the perfect outing for the hot summer days: cool waters and nature everywhere!

Through Castelnuovo Berardenga's way
From Villa Arceno, a large neoclassical villa with a park and a lake in English style, we'll walk to Montalto's castle and to Abbadia Monastero, with the beautiful belltower; we are by Castelnuovo Berardenga, so named from the noble Frank Berardo, that exercised his power on these lands in the tenth century: in short, the least usual village of the most known Siennese Chianti.

The last hills made of clay ("biancane")
Two steps away from Siena there's a pretty enchanted world: it consists of the "biancane" (small hills of clay) of Leonina, an ancient fortress on the northern boundaries of the area of

Siennese Claylands. It' a lunar landscape by now almost destroyed by the today's agricolture. Now, the remains of this world are strictly protected. Why? Easy to answer: too fine!

Through marble and chestnut trees
An interesting walk across the woody slopes of Montagnola Senese, in search of anthropic and natural factors that shaped the present look of this fascinating territory. Among marble quarries and chestnut woods, among old shrines and pasturing pigs, the tour will run through the ancient hamlets of Simignano, Molli and Gallena, the last one with two remarkable towers, the remains of an old castle. A really fine environment in spite of the heavy modifications it's suffering.

In Merse's valley

Stigliano's towers, the secluded village of Brenna, the watermill of the Ricausa, the fortified nucleus named "Castel che Dio sol sa": immersed in a sea of vegetation, we'll go through one of the most woody and untouched zones of Siena's provincia. And, if the weather is good, we'll crown our excursion with a sparkling bath in Merse's river at the point of an ancient ruined dam turned into an unusual hydromassage.

Thermal Springs In Siena

The province of Siena is rich in thermal springs which are often overlooked, as the area is most famous for its architecture, art, history, food and wine. There is so much to choose from when visiting the area of Siena, but a day at some of the area's "terme" is a highlight that one may not want to miss.

The "Terme di Siena" are beautiful and unique, and combined with the area's favorable climate and incredible scenery, it is easy to understand why they attract so many visitors each year. The peaceful landscape and evironment enhance the beneficial effects of the waters. The "terme" also have many therapeutic and healing properties. One can choose from beauty treatments, rehabilitation and fitness, diet, and treatments for respiratory illnesses amongst many things.

Baths and spas in Italy date back to the time of the Etruscans and Romans, when thermal waters were an essential element in a town. In addition to interest in Italy's spas for beauty and health care reasons, their proximity to great centers of art makes the spa resorts excellent bases for cultural excursions. There are many spas to choose from, located in Rapolano, Bagni delle Galleraie, Bagni di Petriolo, San Filippo, Vignoni,

Chianciano, Montepulciano, Fonteverde and San Giovanni di Rapolano.

One of the areas most picturesque place is Terme Bagno Vignoni:

Bagno Vignoni
The town of Bagno Vignoni is located in the Orcia Valley, with a panorama of rocks and castles surrounding it. The springs of the beautiful town square, contain hot spring waters rich in sodium chloride, calcium and iron carbonates, high radioactive calcium, magnesium and sodium sulphates. It is said that St. Catherine and Lorenzo dei Medici were healed by these waters. On the edge of the town, there is a stone culvert where the hot water runs. You take off your shoes and put your feet in. After a long hike it is great. The water is very hot and full of minerals.

Terme di Bagno Vignoni
Address: Bagno Vignoni
Opening Times: From June to September
Phone: (+39) 0577 887365
More info: Email

Terme San Filippo

Terme San Filippo is one of the most spectacular thermal areas in Tuscany, with a wonderful landscape, in the province of Siena and inside the Orcia Valley Park.

Only 60 km far from Siena you can find a Hotel, a Restaurant, a Wellness Centre, a Spa and a thermal pool, a resort located in a green park, inside a quiet natural area with the beautiful Tuscan landscape.

Terre Di Siena

While in Siena or Tuscany, take some days to visit the surrounding areas! Discover the Terre di Siena!

We created a new section dedicated to the wonderful Terre di Siena in Tuscany (Lands of Siena), many of which have been declared UNESCO heritage site.

Terre di Siena have been the scenary for many important movies, like: Zeffirelli's "Brother Sun, Sister Moon" and "Tea with Mussolini ", Bertolucci's "Stealing Beauty", Michael Hoffman's "A Midsummer Night's Dream", Antony Minghella "The English Patient", Andrej Tarkovskij's Nostalgia (the late scene).

Chianti, Tuscany

Chianti is a hillside that rises between 250 and 800 meters above sea level, with slopes also considerable, and largely covered by forests. The territory lies between the provinces of Florence and Siena.

It's famous all around the world to be the land of Chianti Wines, one of the most famous Tuscan wines label.

Chianti has always been, and still is, a wine producing area, that's why you can find many wineries, vineyards and olive trees around. The wine production is a tradition that has ancient roots: the first notarial document which talk about Chianti wines dates back to 1398.

Besides the charm of the countryside that defines the beautiful landscape of the area, you will also find various historical castels, churches, towns and villages dotted around the place. The Chianti was founded by Etruscans and civilized by Romans. In medieval times was scene of battles between Siena and Florence, and that's because in Chianti you can find many towers and castles, abbeys and villages, which were transformed into villas and residences in peacetime.

You can reach and travel Chianti area by foot, mountain bike or horse, but also driving around by car from one village to another, passing by various farmhouses and castels.

Chianti Classico includes the entire municipalities of Castellina in Chianti, Gaiole in Chianti, Radda in Chianti, and partly those of Castelnuovo Berardenga, Poggibonsi, Barberino Val d'Elsa, San Casciano and Tavarnelle Val di Pesa.

Thanks to its peaceful environment, many people from all around the world chose to live in Chianti, between them we can find famous actors and directors, or singers like Sting.

Since almost half of the area is covered with woods, it is a great place to do some outdoor activities, but of course, the most important thing to do while in Chianti is to enjoy some of the high quality food and wine products where this region has become so famous for!

Crete Senesi

Crete Senesi, which literally means Siennese Clays, is the name of the area to the south of Siena. This is a great place to go to if you are looking for some peaceful time. This is an area mainly characterised by pure and untouched nature; hills, woods, waters and a semi-desert, breaking up the green landscape that is typical of Tuscany.

As you can see in the picture at the end of the page the clays appeared as a lunar landscape; this area was covered by sea about 2,5 million years ago.

A great amount of picturesque villages can also be found here, however. A good example of such a village would be Asciano, where you will find a variety of historical monuments. But also Buonconvento, Monteroni d'Arbia, Rapolano Terme and San Giovanni d'Asso are worth a visit.

In this area you can find several spa's as well, for some extra relaxation. In other words Crete Senesi is the perfect place to stop your mind just for a while and to forget about the rest of the world for a couple of days.

Asciano
The village preserves its historic center in the ancient medieval structure. It's located in the heart of Crete Senesi, close to Desert Accona.

Its origin follows the myth of Romulus and Remus: the legend told that the sons of Remus, Senio and Aschio fled from Rome to escape hatred uncle founder of Rome Romulus, Senio refuging on the banks of Tressa river and creating Siena, and Aschio on the banks of Ombrone river founding Asciano.

In reality Asciano was founded under Siena control to which it remained always faithful, like in the Montaperti historic battle in 1260, when thanks to Asciano, Siena won against Florence. Merged first with Medici's possession and later to the Grand Duchy of Tuscany, it followed the events of the other Tuscan territories.

Places of interest to visit in Asciano are: the Collegiate Church of St. Agatha, the Etruscan Museum, the San Lorenzo church, the Museum of Sacred Art (with works by Lorenzetti "San Michele Arcangelo" and "Madonna col Bambino").

Monte Oliveto Maggiore
The Abbey was founded in 1313 by Bernardo Tolomei and played an important role during the Renaissance not only as a religious center but also as a place of economic and cultural exchange.

Today, it is still an active religious center run by the Benedictines, and it collects inside, valuable manuscripts and scrolls restored by monks. It's the seat of the "Istituto di restauro del libro" (Book Restoration Institute).

On the road that leads to the Abbey you will find tall cypresses that, standing in the desert of the Crete Senesi, create a spectacular landscape.

Montaperti
It is renowned for the famous battle of 1260 between Florence and Siena, won by the latter, to which a memorial pyramid is dedicated. The battle is mentioned by Dante in the tenth chapter of the Divine Comedy's "Hell".

Buonconvento
Buonconvento is a historical village that lies in the Ombrone valley. Its history is linked to the history of Siena until the fall of the latter and the annexation to the Medici Grand Duchy in 1554.

It keeps intact the fourteenth century walls, as well as some features of the medieval village, as the "chiasso buio" (literally blind alley), a road paved with medieval arches tunnel.
Attractions: Palace Podestarile with the 25 arms of the old mayors, the Town Hall and Taja Palace, Palazzo Borghese, Palazzo del Glorione, the Oratory of St. Sebastian and the Church of SS. Peter and Paul, the Sacred Art Museum of the Val d'Arbia housed in a 18th century Palazzo Ricci-Socini (which

preserves important works, including those of Duccio di Boninsegna).

It's considered to be one of the most beautiful towns in Italy

Monteroni d'Arbia
The ancient village on the border of the Crete Senesi was founded in the 13th century, and it was, until 1810, a Podestà of Buonconvento property. It has grown around the Hospital of Santa Maria della Scala that built a fortified mill in '300 .

During the war between Florence and Siena, the village was attacked and, consequently, annexed to the Grand Duchy of Florence.

The name was inspired by nearby Mount "Roni", while Arbia is the torrent that flows through the town.

Rapolano Terme
The small village is located between Val di Chiana and Chianti and is famous for its spa waters of the San Giovanni and Ancient Queriolaia Baths. The thermal waters have been known since antiquity, as testified by the ruins of an Imperial Roman bath complex, and are famous for having hosted Giuseppe Garibaldi, who took refuge there to heal the wound in the Battle of Aspromonte.

The structure of the country is affected by the quarries of travertine and marble, which one time helped to increase local economy.

Rapolano waters, which have a temperature of about 39 ° C (37,4F), are sulphurous-bicarbonate-calcium waters.

San Giovanni d'Asso
This small village, inhabited since ancient times, completely surrounds the castle of San Giovanni and is crossed by the River Asso.

The origin of the village dates back to Etruscans, while the development of the city, like testified by the buildings style, was in the Middle Ages.

In the castle of St. John, the highest point of the country, the Museum of truffle was created .

Attractions in San Giovanni d'Asso: Castle of St John, Castle Montisi (on Monte Ghisi), the castles Accarigi and Castelverdelli, the Parish of St. John the Baptist, the Church of San Pietro in Villore.

Events: the carousel of Simon in August, when four horsemen (one for every districts of Montisi) try to hit a target with a spear, the festival of crackles on the first Sunday after Easter.

The white truffle is one of the characteristic flavors of the Crete Senesi, so that in autumn there's a traveling exhibition of white truffle in some countries of Crete: San Giovanni d'Asso, Petroio, Montisi, Asciano, Buonconvento, Monteroni d'Arbia, Serre Rapolano between Crete and the Val d'Orcia

Monte Amiata

Amiata is the name of the Volcano Monte Amiata, which is 1732 m high - the second highest volcano in Italy after the Etna. Even though its last eruption was about 180,000 years ago, still today it heats the surrounding thermal baths, such as Bagno Vignoni or Bagni San Fillippo, and even the more distant like Petriolo and Saturnia.

Thanks to its altitude, Amiata Mountain has also become one of the most important and popular skiing resorts in Tuscany and surroundings. Tourism is therefore becoming an increasing source of income, besides wood and chestnuts.

The Mountain stands between Valdorcia and Maremma and from there you can enjoy an incomparable landscape of Southern Tuscany.

Abbadia San Salvatore and the Benedictine Abbey of San Salvatore

It's famous as an holiday center both in summer and winter time. Grown around the Abbey of St. Salvatore it maintains the ancient medieval town, with streets, houses and walls.

The Mine of Abbadia which in the past provided a strong economic growth to the area but also problems for working conditions, is now a mining museum.

On the occasion of the famous festival "Fiaccole della Notte di Natale", (on Christmas Eve), Abbadia San Salvatore turns into a magic village full of torches and bonfires. During this night, thirty 5 m tall stacks of wood are burned, while a torchlight procession leads torches to piles for ignition and everybody sings Christmas' songs. The bonfires burn until morning and the party lasts all night long.

Abbey of San Salvatore

For thousands years, the Abbey has been a religious complex belonged to both Benedictines and Cistercians and represented an important center of power, whose ruins of the Church and the Crypt are visible still today. Fallen into decline, it became Siena's property in 1347 and annexed to Florence in 1559.

With the Grand Duke Leopold 2nd, the monastery was suppressed and its treasures were transferred to Florence. In 1939, a community of Benedictines takes possession of the Abbey.

Bagni San Filippo
The Thermal Baths are popular since the Middle Ages, visited by many famous people, including members of the Medici family.

Arcidosso
Arcidosso is a village which rises 679 meters above sea level. The highest point is the Aldobrandesco castle, built around 1000. Around this castle, Arcidosso then began to develop. The name of the castle comes from the family who owned Arcidosso in the 12th - 14th century: the Aldobrandeschi, fell after a long siege of Siena in 1331. To see: the sanctuary of Our Lady Crowned, the church of Santa Maria di Lamulas.

Santa Fiora
It takes its name from the river Fiora, which stands here and now supplies water to the entire Southern Tuscany.

The Lords of Santa Fiora were the Aldobrandeschi, who in 1082 began the construction of a castle (Castle of St. Florian) and its walls.

Near the source of the river Fiora, you can find a pond surrounded by a park, where today you can fish and relax in the luxuriant nature, but once it was part of the garden belonging to Palazzo Sforza-Cesarini (Lords of Santa Fiora after the Aldobrandeschi).

Places to visit: Museum of the mines, the Parish Church with ceramics by Andrea della Robbia.

Events: in recent years, Santa Fiora has become famous for hosting musical events, including some important events of symphonic music, jazz and ethnic concerts.

Val Di Chiana

Val di Chiana is located to the eastern border of Val d'Orcia and touches the region of Umbria to the south. It is a valley covering an area of about 2300 km2 with an average altitude of 405 meters. It has one of the most fertile grounds of the country, feature which is mainly due to the presence of numerous man-made channels and streams which were dug over the past centuries.

This is a land famous for its thermal baths, located in many Val di Chiana's cities like: Chianciano, Montepulciano, San Casciano dei Bagni, Chiusi, Cetona and Trequanda.

Val di Chiana is a great place for those who like outdoor activities, such as trekking, horseback riding or mountain biking. But for those looking for culture and history, this area has something to offer as well. Here you will find for example, 'La rocca longobarda di Civitella', which was destroyed during a bombing in 1944 and never reconstructed, or the National Archaeological Museum Gaio Cilnio Mecenate in Arezzo.

Located on top of a hill you will find Montepulciano, the largest municipality of Val di Chiana. As this municipality is surrounded by fortifications and several Renaissance palaces and churches, a visit there will represent a sort of journey back in time. In other words, Val di Chiana is definitely worth a visit!

Here originate the Chianina, a breed of cattle from which the famous "Bistecca alla fiorentina" (Florentine steak) derives.

Cetona

The medieval village of Cetona, located in the southern east province of Siena, still preserves its ancient origins. It stands on a hill with a fortress (Rocca) situated at the highest point of Monte Cetona (1148 meters above sea level) surrounded by pine trees and cypresses. In Cetona there are still traces of the ancient walls.

To visit: The Archaeological Natural Park in the Belverde-Biancheto Area, where you can see traces of ancient settlements dating back to prehistory.

Chianciano Terme

Situated at the border between Umbria and Tuscany, Chianciano Terme has always been famous for the healing properties of its mineral waters, known since the time of the Etruscans and Romans. Etruscan origins are demonstrated by important findings, like paintings and objects, including about 70 canopic jars inside the imposing necropolis (more than 700 tombs so far discovered) near the city.

Chianciano is located between Val di Chiana and Val d'Orcia.

Chianciano Vecchia stands on a hill, partly surrounded by medieval walls. Still retains part of its ancient urban plan.

The new village, however, has grown up around the famous Terme, among which we mention: the Acquasanta, Park Fucoli Park Baths of St. Helena, the Thermal Baths of the sensory and Sillene.

Chiusi

Chiusi, which extends between the ValdiChiana and Val d'Orcia in southern Tuscany border with Umbria, is worldwide famous for its Etruscan origins: it was, in fact, one of the 12 cities comprising the Etruscan dodecapoli and one of the oldest known Etruscan cities.

Today is a very important archaeological site, famous for its Etruscan findings. Many of the finds are collected at the National Etruscan Museum of Archaeology, as well as the Etruscan tombs called "della Pellegrina" (Pilgrim's Tomb) and "del Leone" (Lion's Tomb). It is possibile to walk inside the Labyrinth of King Porsenna, king of Etruria lived in the fifth century BC who, according to the legend, wanted his tomb at the center of a maze that lies beneath the city. In fact the tunnels that run in the city's underground where in the past streets that led to tanks used for the collection of rainwater. No trace of the tomb of King Porsenna was found, although hopes are not completely exhausted because only a small part of the underground galleries have been recovered, yet, while the corridors digged into the tuff sandstone run under the whole city. They were filled with several materials by Romans and slowly brought to light only during the twentieth century.

Places to visit: in addition to the National Archaeological Museum and the Etruscan tombs already mentioned, the Tomb of the Monkey (della Scimmia), the Civic Museum and the Cathedral Museum, which gives access to the Labyrinth of Porsenna (with guided tour offered). A few miles from town there's a beautiful lake where you can see different species of birds.

Sinalunga

Sinalunga extends between the Val di Chiana and Val Ombrone and is divided into two parts: the village at the top and the Parish at the bottom.

inalunga is well known for its culinary products, including wine, oil and Chianina beef, used for the famous Florentine steak.

Sinalunga was an Etruscan settlement of Chiusi lucumonia; you will find there, remains of an ancient city walls dating back to the medieval time and some towers in the south-east.

Trequanda

Trequanda stands on a hill between Val di Chiana and Asso Valley. It has Etruscan origins, even if the main development occurred in the Middle Ages, when the Cacciaconti Castle was built, that still exists and around which the village has expanded. Grown under the influence of Siena, Trequanda fell, together with Siena, under the Florentine Republic of Medici, in 1554.

Early in the nineteenth century the territory was invaded and occupied by the French troops led by Napoleon Bonaparte, and annexed, then, to the Grand Duchy of Tuscany, in 1815, and with this to the Italian Kingdom in 1861.

Attractions in Trequanda: the Church of Saints Peter and Andrew, the old villages of Petroio and Castelmuzio with the beautiful Romanesque parish church of Santo Stefano.

The town was awarded with the prestigious Orange Flag of the Italian Touring Club, a symbol used to reward some inland locations selected and certified by the Touring for their particular features.

Trequanda is one the countries that are on the "Nature Train" route, a train that, every Sunday from May to October, crosses the southern countryside of Siena, through the valleys of Arbia and Orcia and area of the Crete Senesi.

Montepulciano

Montepulciano is situated on the top of a hill between Val di Chiana and Val d'Orcia, and is the largest municipality of Val di Chiana. Founded by the Etruscans, the popular tradition located in Montepulciano, a sort of summer residence of King Porsenna.

Val D'elsa

Val d'Elsa, borrowing its name from the river Elsa, is located in the heart of Tuscany close to the cities of Siena, Florence and Volterra. Today it is mostly appreciated for its unspoiled nature and well known for the production of crystal glassware and art (15% of the worlds and 98% of Italy's production).

We suggest to visit:

Colle Val d'Elsa

Colle Val d'Elsa is a village perched on a high hill and divided into two zones: "High Colle" and "low Colle".

The city is mentioned in the Italian history for the famous battle of Colle di Val d'Elsa that decreed the victory of the Florentine and Colle's Guelphs against Sienise Ghibellines. The battle took place between 16 and 17 June 1269.

Colle Val d'Elsa is the birthplace of Arnolfo di Cambio, to whom is dedicated the main square. Colle Val d'Elsa is connected by bus to Florence and Siena.

Events in Colle Val d'Elsa:

Cristallo tra le mura

The event is dedicated to the crystal produced at Colle and takes place every year in the first three weekends of September. During the event, you can see demonstrations of crystal working with different techniques: hot, cold, carving, engraving and grinding. Besides this there are stands with food and wine, wine tasting and the opening of the extraordinary museums.

LiberaCollArte

Day's art: from 10 am until late at night there are stands with local and international crafts, theater, art installations, street musicians and a great final concert with famous artists of the Italian music scene. LiberaCollArte is held every year in September.

Casole d'Elsa
Casole d'Elsa is a medieval village that rises along the valley of the Elsa river.

It's placed on a hill at 417m above sea level, from which you can enjoy a beautiful landscape of the Elsa Valley and the surrounding campaign.

Founded by Etruscans, it was controlled by the bishop of Volterra until the 13th century when, after a period of free municipality, fell under the Siena control after a long siege.

Despite several uprisings, Casole remained a Siena possession until 1554, when it was annexed to the Florence property under the rule of the Medici family. In this time an economic development started, and continued even under the Lorraine.

Among the several events taking place in Casole you will find the Palio di Casole, on the second Sunday of July (St. Isidore). This is a horse race, on a dirt road, with uphill. It 'a "long run" prize where the starting point does not match with that of arrival.

During the week before the Palio in the districts evening parties and dinners are organized.

Attractions: The Collegiate Church of Santa Maria Assunta, the praetorian palace, Rocca Senese (nowadays the town hall).

To get to Casole d'Elsa take the road Siena -Florence and exit Colle Val d'Elsa Nort, then turn left towards Casole d'Elsa (direction: Volterra).

San Gimignano

San Gimignano is a medieval village perched on a hill over 300m above sea level, famous for its towers dominating the whole valley.

The construction of the towers dates back from the 11th to the 13th century. In this period the economy was flourishing and the city was politically independent, the urban aristocracy that had formed in the city wanted to demonstrate their political and social supremacy, and building up 72 towers.

This prosperous period ended in 1300 after a major famine and the spread of Black Death, when San Gimignano gave up its independence and surrendered voluntarily to Florence.

14 of the ancient 72 towers are still standing, others are ruins, but still visible. The Torre del Podestà (also called Rognosa), 51 meters high, is the oldest. The Torre Grossa, for only 3 cm, is the highest.

Below is a list of the towers of San Gimignano:

- two Torri degli Ardinghelli
- Torre dei Becci
- Torre Campatelli
- Torre Chigi
- Torre dei Cugnanesi
- Torre del Diavolo
- Torre Ficherelli o Ficarelli
- Torre Grossa
- Torre di Palazzo Pellari
- Torre Pettini
- Torre Rognosa
- two Torri dei Salvucci

To these we can add two case-torri (towerhouses): the bell tower of the Collegiate and the Torre Pesciolini.

San Gimignano maintains its aspect reminding to 13 and 14 centuries and in 1990 the Old Town was been declared a UNESCO World Heritage Site.

If you are in Florence and want to visit Siena and San Gimignano we suggest you to visit: tour in Siena and San Gimignano

Val D'orcia

Val d'Orcia, also written as Valdorcia, is located south of Crete and extends from the hills south of Siena to Monte Amiata. It comprises grain fields, carefully-cultivated hills, streams and several medieval towns and villages such as Pienza, which was completely rebuilt in the mid 15th century, Montalcino, a hill town well-known for its red Brunello wine and Radicofani.

These municipalities, more Castiglione d'Orcia and San Quirico d'Orciaconstitute the "Parco artistico, naturale e culturale della Val d'Orcia" (artistic, natural and cultural Park of the Val d'Orcia).

This area has become famous for the absolute beauty of its landscapes. This could be seen in the many movies that have been filmed here. Just to name a few: The English patient, the Gladiator, Under The Tuscan Sun and Romeo and Juliet are all movies that made use of the beautiful Tuscan scenery in Val d'Orcia. In 2004 Val d'Orcia was even added to the UNESCO list of World Heritage Sites.

There are several bike or walk routes to be followed, to admire the beautiful landscape, but also to see the several churches of the area such as the Church of St Anna or the Church of St Antimo.

We suggest to visit:

Pienza

Pienza is a Renaissance town, famous for its design. The works which completely transfigurated Pienza in 15th century were wanted by the most famous Pienza inhabitant: Enea Silvio Piccolomini, elevated to Pope Pius II in 1458.

He wanted the ancient Castello di Corsignano as a Papal residence, changing it and Pienza in Renaissance style, inspired to a model of "ideal city" and to an utopia of ideal living and governing, where people could live in peace, in a balance of man and nature. The renovation was made under the supervision of Bernardo Rossellino and Leon Battista Alberti.

To visit in Pienza: Palazzo Piccolomini, the Duomo (Cattedrale dell'Assunta) which houses several Sienese Renaissance artists paintings, Palazzo Borgia, Palazzo Comunale.

How to reach Pienza: from Siena take direction Monteroni - Buonconvento. After Buonconvento, take direction San Quirico d' Orcia and in San Quirico follow for Pienza.

Monticchiello

Monticchiello is a small town in the heart of Val d'Orcia, near Pienza.

The medieval center is still visible in many remains of fortifications, that represent real symbols of its most flourishing period, under the Republic of Siena: the walls and towers, the main entrance to the city, the fortress, the twelfth-century Church of St. Leonard and Christopher with frescoes belonging to the fourteenth and fifteenth century.

The center lost its strategic importance after the fall of the Sienese Republic and the annexation to the Republic of Florence.

Today Monticchiello is famous for its "Poor Theatre" (Teatro Povero), a manifestation of street theater designed and developed entirely by locals, who deal with the writing of stories based on the life of the village and the history of Monticchiello, the creation of sets and composition of music. Such plays are then performed by the inhabitants themselves. The shows take place from mid July to mid August, every evening except on Monday.

Montalcino

San Quirico d'Orcia
The ancient village situated in the north of Val d'Orcia has Etruscan origins. Possession of Siena since 1256 has kept intact its medieval origins.

There you can admire beautiful Renaissance buildings, medieval walls, the Collegiate Church of Saints Quirico and Julietta, the beautiful Park Leonini gardens (Horti Leonini).

Montalcino is known all around the world, especially thanks to its wine, the famous "Brunello di Montalcino".

The town, which takes its name from the many oaks (Montalcino = mountain of oaks) widespread in the area and represented in the coat of arms, is located between the Crete Senesi and the Val d'Orcia, close to Pienza and Monte Amiata.

"The railway departs from Asciano station and covers two kms before it runs through big valleys with bold viaducts and galleries. On the right a striking view of the outstanding gullies around the Monte Oliveto Maggiore Abbey opens to your eyes.

By Trequanda station the line enters the Asso valley. The train runs through sweet hills whose colours recalls the Siena clay and reaches the town San Giovanni d'Asso overlooked by the Middle Age Castle.

Still plunged in this amazing landscaspe, the line now approaches the monumental Torrenieri-Montalcino station which was built in 1865; beyond it the stretch goes through cultivated fields and comes closer to the Asso stream.

The shape of Montalcino stands out in the distance on the right side of the railway and on its feet green valleys stretch covered by wineyards which give birth to the esteemed wine Brunello. The herds aren't bothered by the train running and browse peacefully in the meadows. Sometimes some wildlife specimen even show up on the sides of the line such us pheasants, hares, foxes, wild pigs and fallow deer.

After passing the Casalta gallery, the line enters the valley Val d'Orcia and arrives in the little town Monte Amiata Scalo.

It then approches the stony bed of the river and they almost overlap. For a short track you can discern on the right the village Castelnuovo dell'Abate which arose near the old Abbey of Sant'Antimo, while on the left the mountain dominates and you can perceive the soft contours of the villages lying on its slopes.

The valley widens out. Here the railway runs through the wineyards and orchards of Villa Banfi and then arrives in Sant'Angelo-Cinigiano station. The small town Sant'Angelo Scalo has arisen around this station.

Treno Natura near Lucignano d'Arbia (picture by Benedetto Sabatini) The train keeps on running along the Orcia valley heading for the Maremma region, it passes under the Poggio le Mura Castle where the glas museum has its seat, crosses the Ombrone river and approches Monte Antico station.

300 meters ahead the Orcia river ends its run which started many kilometers before between Radicofani Rock and the Cetona Mountain. Its clear waters join those of the Ombrone river and flow together slowly to the sea.

Our line meets the one coming from Siena through Buonconvento and it then joins the Tirrenica Railway under the Middle Age village Montepescali".

Val Di Merse

Val di Merse is located in the western edge of Siena and in the southern border of Val d'Elsa, between the rivers Farma and Merse (from which it takes its name as well). It is famous for its beautiful landscapes, its unspoilt nature and the healing powers of the many waters of Val di Merse.

Some of the villages in this area that are definitely worth a visit are Monticiano, Chiusdino, Murlo and Sovicille, such small villages that you will have the opportunity to visit at least a couple of them on the same day.

If you look between the woods of Val di Merse you will also find a numerous amount of medieval hamlets and castels hiding between the trees

Merse River

The river Merse originates in the province of Grosseto and flows across a tortuous path until it reaches the Siena area, passing near the villages of Sovicille, Monticiano, Murlo and Chiusdino.

The river, which in many places is only accessible by foot, is suitable for making beautiful bathrooms, fully immersed in the Tuscan countryside. The Merse is one of the last refuges of the otter.

The Merse valley is perfect for trekking and for most adventurous, it's possible to canoe down the river from the Abbey of San Galgano to the confluence with the Ombrone.

Murlo: the land of Etruscans

Murlo is a beautiful medieval town, built on a hill high 300m above sea level and completely enclosed by ancient walls, then overlapped by a circle of houses.

Founded by the Etruscans, Murlo shows great evidence of their civilization, as can be seen in the archaeological site of Poggio Civitate for example, where, thanks to some American

Universities, lots of materials belonging to Etruscans have been discovered.

The materials found are visible in the Etruscan Antiquarium Museum of Poggio Civitate. According to some genetic studies, the population of Murlo could be the most direct descendants of the Etruscans.

Chiusdino and the Sword in the Stone

Chiusdino is a Medieval village perched on a metalliferous hill 564 mt above sea level, between Val di Farma and the upper valley of Merse River.

Its medieval walls and urban plan are intact. They are characterized by narrow streets with low stone houses concentric to the town center.

The origins are Lombard, while in the Middle Ages was a property of the Volterra Bishops, until 1215 when, after a period of struggle, was annexed to Siena. Thus began a prosperous period, that continued with the domination of the Medici Family from Florence, under which several monasteries and abbey were constructed.

Chiusdino Associations promote various fairs and festivals during the summer. Among these in early September there's the Festival of sweet, with tasting of local wine and sweets.

Monuments to visit: Church of St. Sebastian, Chiesa della Compagnia di San Galgano, which is near the birthplace of Saint Galgano Guidotti (1148 - 1181), Castle Miralduolo, Lenzi Palaces

Abbazia di San Galgano and Eremo di Monte Siepi

San Galgano was born in Chiusdino in 1148. 30 years later, after a life devoted to luxury, he chose to retire in penance on Monte Siepi. Here, in order to show his repentance, he plunged his sword into a rock. In this same place the Romanesque church of Monte Siepi (Eremo di Monte Siepi) was built, where it is possible to see, yet, the "Sword in the Stone".

Someone argues that is precisely the Sword in the Stone of the myth of King Arthur.

A few years after the death of San Galgano, an Abbey was built by the Cistercians, in the valley of Monte Siepi. Abandoned at the end of '400 it fell into ruin in the 18th century until the late '800, when it was restored by consolidating the existing. Today it is a picturesque ceiling open ruin (as you can see in the picture), as the roof collapsed under the bell tower fall on 1786.

Monticiano and Bagni di Petriolo.

The town of Monticiano is located on a hill 375mt above sea level.

Founded by the bishop of Volterra, Monticiano was invaded by Siena in the late thirteenth century: after the defeat of Colle Val d'Elsa, in 1269, Sienese occupied the town and destroied the castle's walls for giving refuge to the Ghibellines traitors. In 1554, it was then attached to the Grand Duchy of Tuscany, after Florence's victory over Siena. Thus began in Monticiano a flourishing period, with the erection of noble palaces.

During the Second World War it was an important area of partisan guerrilla operations, a basis for the Sienese partisan groups.

Among the most important monuments to visit: the Church of St. Augustine, Abbey of San Galgano, the Parish of Saints Giusto and Clemente, Palace Callian and Thermal baths of Petrolio.

Petriolo Baths (Thermal baths)

The Petriolo thermae (fortified thermal baths) are located in the region of Monticiano, very close to the main road that connects Siena to Grosseto. At km 27 (coming from Siena) there's a little street that brings directly both to the equipped spa and hotels and to the open air thermal baths (free). These last flow into the river Farma and the result is a fantastic place where you can experience the transition from hot thermal waters (about 43 °C - 109.4 F) to the cold waters of the river, very good for circulation.

The Petriolo thermae were known since Roman times; in 1400 was built a stone spa and the thermal baths became popular and frequented by the Medici family.

The Petriolo waters are sulfide-sulfate-bicarbonate-alkaline-earthy, recognized as mineral waters.

Sovicille

Sovicille is a village located just a few kilometers far from Siena, with a beautiful medieval historical center, visible for the walls and some stone houses and streets. Founded around year 1000 by the Bishop of Siena, it became a free municipality in the 13th century, but kept to be reason of conflict among the neighboring towns and was constantly invaded and besieged until 1554, when it was annexed to the Medici's family properties, finally starting a flourishing period.

After Lorraine period, the area was invaded by Napoleon's troops which remained until the Treaty of Vienna (1814) that sanctioned the return to the Grand Duchy of Tuscany.

In 1861 it was annexed with the entire Grand Duchy to the Kingdom of Italy. To visit: the church of San Lorenzo with its neo-gothic architecture.

Il Ponte della Pia

The bridge known as "Ponte della Pia" has Roman origin, but was rebuilt in the Middle Ages. It joins the two banks of the torrent Rosia and in the past was a crucial bridge that united the provinces of Siena and Grosseto. The side parapets were destroyed by German tanks during the Second World War, so that it is possible to cross it just by foot today.

For the legend every night of full moon appears on the bridge the ghost of Countess Pia de' Tolomei, which was thrown by her second husband from the cliff where there was the Castel di Pietra in Maremma, today known as "the jump of the

Countess". The Lady is mentioned by Dante in the Canto V of Purgatory.

Castello di Montarrenti

The area Montarrenti was established as a village of huts in the 7th and 8th centuries and then transformed into a castle, as a center for the collection of agricultural products.

The area consisted of the castle with two palaces (because there still are two towers), the Church of Santa Maria and a village inhabited by farmers, rather populated until the annexation to the Republic of Siena in 1217.

The Castle, probably abandoned due to the closure of silver mines, went gradually to ruin, and today only two towers stand and some remains of the walls.

Today the castle houses the astronomical observatory operated by Unione Astrofili Senesi and CAI (Italian Alpine Club).

To reach the Castle: from Siena take the road 73 (statale Senese Aretina), beyond the village of Rosia almost until the junction with road 541 (statale Traversa Maremmana) from which it's possibile to reach Colle Val d'Elsa.

Restaurants In Siena

Eating and Drinking
Siena cooking is characterized by cereals, pulses, herbs, game and pork, in particular the famous cinta senese, a wonderful breed of pigs that is bred only in Chianti.

One of the most typical products in this area are cold meats such as soppressata, finocchiona and capocolli, in addition to other specialties made from wild boar meat. The area is also famous for cheeses such as cacio pecorino, from the Siena clay lands and marzolino.

Extra virgin olive oil is also a typical product of the Siena hills: This oil, with its unmistakable fruity aroma, is produced using the olives that grow in the Chianti countryside. It is used in all traditional Siena dishes, especially crude so that its particular taste can be noted.

A typical Siena lunch or dinner may begin with an hors d'oeuvre of chicken liver crostini, or game crostini, followed by lentil soup with pheasant, Siena bean soup or frog soup, in addition to the classic Ribollita and pasta with chick peas. Siena restaurants and trattorias offer various choices for the second course – from hare to sweet and sour wild boar, roast pork, which can also be served cold with garlic and rosemary.

As dessert we recommend two sweets that belong to the famous Siena confectionery tradition: panforte and ricciarelli. Panforte is an ancient sweet, used for many centuries only for religious ceremonies. This filling sweet, that is typically eaten at Christmas, is prepared with flour, almonds, candied fruit, dry fruit and spices, all laid on a thin wafer.

Ricciarelli are lozenge-shaped almond biscuits made by mixing almond paste, honey and vanilla and baked in the over to give them their typical crunchy outer layer.

We shall end this section with a mention of wine, a jewel in the crown of the Tuscany region. Wine production in the Chianti countryside goes back to ancient times: some Etruscan finds have shown that grapes were already grown at that time, but Chianti was first associated with wine starting in 1404. Over the centuries, the wine known as Chianti Classico has become more and more famous in Italy and abroad. Some of the most famous wines are Nobile di Montepulciano, Rosso di Montalcino and the exceptional Brunello di Montalcino, produced from a Sangiovese vine in the borough of

Montalcino, which is aged for 4 years at least in oak or chestnut casks. Today, 5 different DOCG wines and 12 DOC wines are produced in the area around Siena.

Dining Out In Siena
Antica Trattoria Papei

A popular trattoria with outdoor seating at Piazza del Mercato, and traditional Senese dishes such as fresh pasta with wild boar sauce, ravioli in sage butter sauce, tripe, bruschetta, etc.

Address: Piazza del Mercato, 6

Phone: 0577 280894

Trattoria Fontenuova

This piceria is a favorite of locals and offers fresh hand made pici, with a variety of sauces such as ragu, sausage or cheese, pepper and herbs. Grilled meats, vegetables and fresh desserts of the day are also offered. Prices are very reasonable and the table wine is worth the visit.

Address: Piazzetta Ovile 9/10

Phone: 0577 49351

Osteria del Ficomezzo

Dishes offered include Tagliata and hand made pasta dishes. Over 100 local, Italian and foreign wines offered.

Address: Via dei Termini, 71

Phone: 0577 222384

Due Porte

A few minutes from Piazza del Campo, the Due Porte Pizzeria offers fresh fish dishes, barbecued meats, and pizzas baked in a wood burning oven. The charming veranda offers a spectacular view of the Siennese landscape.

Address: Via Stalloreggi, 62

Phone: 0577 221887

Osteria Le Logge

A typical style restaurant which offers a traditional but interesting menu. The owner, Gianni Brunelli, produces an excellent Brunello di Montalcino.

Address: Via del Porrione, 33

Phone: 0577 48013

Ristorante Pizzeria Due Archi

Enjoy pizza from a wood burning oven or traditional Tuscan dishes at this popular spot.

Address: Pian dei Mantellini, 48

Phone: 0577 42277

Il Grattacielo

This is the place where local Sienese still go for lunch. Lunch consists of fresh sausage, salami, local cheeses and salads such as white bean, eggplant, tomato, etc. Enjoy lunch for about 6 or 7 euros, including a glass of the house wine.

Address: Via Pontani 8

Phone: 0577 289326

La Verbena

Located outside the walls of Siena, this restaurant offers meat and fish dishes, as well as delicous pizzas.

Address: Via Pescaia, 53

Phone: 0577 289837

Ristorante La Pizzeria di nonno Mede

This charming pizzeria offers outdoor seating in front of one of Siena's best views -- the Duomo, historical center and the hills of Siena. The menu includes an extensive variety of Pizze, Ciaccini (a specialty of the region), Focaccine Ripiene (stuffed focaccia) and Calzoni. Prices are reasonable, but inquire about the price of your wine before you drink it.

Address: Camporegio, 21

Phone: 0577 247966

Osteria Chiacchera

A comfortable and casual spot with a medeival ambiance, traditional sienese specialties know in italian as "piatti poveri." The menu offers such dishes as Trippa, Pici, Ribollita Soup, and of course the famous cookies of Tuscany, "cantucci," served with the sweet dessert wine of the region, Vin Santo.

Address: Costa di S. Antonio, 4

Phone: 0577 280631

Tea Room

This cafe is a hot spot for students and the young Senese - but only in cold weather months - as it offers hot tea from around the world. A torta of the day is also offered, along with biscotti, liquors and hot chocolates. You can choose from many board games while you sip your tea, or sit back and listen to live music. Be sure to reserve one of the private rooms in advance if you have a group.

Address: Porta Giustizia, 11

Phone: 0577 222753

Vecchia Trattoria Vallerozzi

Located right in the contrada della Lupa, this small restaurant is located on one of Siena's most charming and steepest streets.

There is a tiny spot for outdoor seating, and the trattoria offers typical Tuscan cooking, local salumi, cheese and wine. The location is just minutes from Piazza della Posta.

Address: Via Vallerozzi, 36

Phone: 0577 43435

La Finestra

One of Siena's most popular restaurants, offering delicious local specialties, good atmosphere and friendly service. It is one of the few restaurants located at Piazza del Mercato, with an outdoor veranda and a view of Palazzo Comunale, the Torre del Mangia and the Sienese hills just beyond the Piazza. Dishes with wild boar, truffles and porcini mushrooms are some of the specialties offered.

Address: Piazza del Mercato, 14

Phone: 0477 42093

L'Osteria

A simple osteria located close to the contradas of Brucco and Giraffaa, known as a spot where local Senese frequent. The menu offers traditional pasta, Tuscan bread soups, grilled meats and risotto, and prices are very reasonable.

Address: Via dei Rossi, 79

Phone: 0577 287592

Ristorante- Pizzeria "Fontebecci"

This restaurant is located outside the walls of Siena, and serves real authentic Naples style pizza. It can be reached by bus, and is said to be worth the trip!

Address: Via Fiorentina, 133

Phone: 0577 50259

Il Vinaio dell'Eremita di Porta all'Arco

For the lovers of flavors of ancient Siena, this charming vinaio is a great spot to enjoy regional wines and antipasti, cured meats and cheeses, as well as Tuscan specialties.

Address: Via delle Cerchia 2

Phone: 0577 49490

Il Rialto

This traditional restaurant is located a bit "off the beaten path," and offers fresh fish.

Address: Via del Rialto, 4

Phone: 0577 236580

Tullio "ai Tre Cristi"

This restaurant is located in the charming contrada of the

Giraffe and offers Tuscan specialties, with refined and modern presentation. The service is excellent and the wine list is extensive.

Address: Via Provenzano 1/7

Phone: 0577 280608

Top Spots For Aperitivo In Siena

Cacio e Pere

Technically a bar, Cacio e Pere is one of the most buzzing places to be on any given night in Siena. Playing host to local musicians almost every night, it's a prime spot to get a real feel for the lively music scene in the city; all you have to do is stop by for the aperitivo. The atmosphere is decidedly more grungy than many of the other spots on our list, with an almost pub-like feel, but don't be fooled into thinking that it's just for the 20-somethings. It remains an amazing place for cocktails and live music.

70 Via dei Termini, Siena, 53100, Italy

+3905771510727

Caffé la Pizzetta

One of the most vibrant aperitivo scenes in Siena can be found at Caffé la Pizzetta. Located a short walk from the busiest streets of downtown Siena, this spot definitely attracts a younger crowd with DJs and an upbeat, club-like vibe. Drinks are always flowing, and the food buffet is always on point, while customers mingle and dance to the music. What makes Caffé la Pizzetta really special is a sponsorship-type program, special aperitivo nights that fund raise for charities. Caffé la Pizzetta is also one of the only advertised LGBTQ-friendly places for nightlife in the city.

Caffé la Pizzetta, Via Montanini, 52, 53100 Siena, Italy

Café Nannini
Café Nannini is one of the more elegant places for aperitivo, located on Banchi di Sopra for ultimate convenience. The cafe is housed in a beautiful old building with artisan stone and woodwork. In keeping with the upscale feel, the evening aperitivo feels fancy and special. Along with finger foods, you can also order a refreshing gelato or fresh pastry. Because of its prime location and well-known name, Café Nannini can get busy, so prepare to share a table and make some new friends.

24 Via Banchi di Sopra, Siena, Toscana, 53100, Italy

+390577236009

Da Trombicche

Da Trombicche combines fresh ingredients, old recipes, and warm hospitality to create an unforgettable experience. The restaurant has been in its current location in Siena for over 50 years, establishing itself as a mainstay in the local restaurant scene. This truly is a place to relax and wind down, as the restaurant's site describes the atmosphere as casual and familiar. You'll be treated like family when you stop by for aperitivo hour, which always features local products and ingredients, and typical plates from the Senese region.

66 Via delle Terme, Siena, Toscana, 53100, Italy

+390577288089

La Favorita
Though Siena is known for medieval charm and history, La Favorita feels like a little slice of modernity. The cafe's interior features clean lines and neutral colors, making it feel incredibly chic. Upon entering, guests are first greeted by a tempting display of brightly colored gelatos and pastries before reaching the bar to order a drink. From there, grab your beverage of choice and stay upstairs where the action usually is or retreat downstairs to a quieter, more intimate dining area. The restaurant has one of the best outdoor patios in the city, so

visit on a warm summer night to get some fresh air along with your drinks and appetizers.

32 Piazza Giacomo Matteotti, Siena, Toscana, 53100, Italy

+39057741932

La Prosciutteria
Most people are familiar with prosciutto, the cured Italian equivalent of ham. But dining on high-quality prosciutto, with local pecorino, and perhaps a glass of chianti? It's an experience of a lifetime. La Prosciutteria doesn't always serve a dedicated aperitivo hour, but is an excellent place for drinks and a bite to eat. Most popular are their meat and cheese platters, with a sampling of cheeses, salumi, olives, and crostini. It is tucked back on a side street, away from the popular tourist sites in Siena, so is perfect for a quiet and tranquil evening of excellent wine and finger foods that are very typical of the Tuscan region. It is immensely popular with the local residents due to its authenticity and charm.

La Prosciutteria, Via Pantaneto, Angolo Via Magalotti, 53100 Siena, Italy

Le Tre Rane

Le Tre Rane is just a fantastic place to spend an evening in Siena. Hidden off the main paths that most tourists tread, the restaurant has a truly inviting feel. The aperitivo menu is a great way to enjoy the calm atmosphere with a light dinner, but you may find a few surprises here as well. Along with traditional Italian appetizers, Le Tre Rane chefs often serve multiple varieties of sushi, for a little unexpected kick of flavor.

Liberamente Osteria

Piazza del Campo is the heart of Siena and one of its most recognizable landmarks. Liberamente Osteria is just one of many restaurants lining the piazza, and it offers one of the best aperitivo spreads in the city. Expect finger sandwiches, sausages, crostini, and even arancini: warm and gooey, deep-fried balls of rice and cheese. Its location on the edge of the most popular destination in the city can make it busy with tourists at times, but the quality and selection at Liberamente Osteria keeps locals and visitors coming back.

Liberamente Osteria, Piazza Il Campo 27, 53100 Siena, Italy

Osteria Boccon del Prete

Osteria Boccon del Prete is an off-the-beaten-track restaurant that serves the meal of your dreams. This place can get crowded, as it doesn't accommodate more than a few dozen people, but the wait is worth it. Because the aperitivo menu is served buffet-style, you never quite know what you're going to get, but if luck is on your side, you'll get to try the house specialty: a fresh pasta dish with a light, creamy pesto sauce.

17 Via San Pietro, Siena, Toscana, 53100, Italy

+390577280388

Ristorante Alla Speranza
Ristorante Alla Speranza is another excellent place for aperitivo that that sits right on the Piazza del Campo. The view could not get better, with al fresco dining that looks out to the stunning Gaia Fountain and the 318-foot Torre del Mangia. Should you choose to dine inside, you may feel like you stepped back in time; the restaurant's interior feels like a scene from a movie, with ancient brick walls, old stone hearths, and an arched brick ceiling. Enjoy traditional Tuscan specialties while you take in the sites of this unique and beautiful city.

32/36 Il Campo, Siena, Toscana, 53100, Italy

+390577280190

Transportation In Siena

To Get in

By plane

Siena's Ampugnano airport is located 9 km from the city. At the moment, there are no scheduled air services to Siena airport. For additional information tel 0577-392226. A shuttle service connection is currently available between the airport and Piazza Gramsci TRA-IN (tel. 0577-204224).

Most travellers arriving by plane will land at airports in Florence or Pisa. Buses of the Sena line connect Siena with the Bologna Marconi airport (twice daily, 2.5 hours), a favorite with the discount carriers. There is also a bus link to Pisa airport.

By car

From the north, take the Chiantigiana from Florence (SS 222 - 72 km) that elegantly crosses the hills of Chianti or the highway (SS 2 superstrada Siena/Firenze - 68 km). From the south, Siena can be reached by taking the Autoway from Rome (A1 Roma-Firenze, exit Valdichiana), turning right on state highway #326 (Bettolle-Siena - 240 km). Relatively cheap parking can be found near Fortezza Medicea, northwest of the city stadium - and around it.

By train

From the north, trains go about hourly directly from Florence to Siena, and otherwise it is possible to take any train that stops in Empoli and find train connections from Empoli to Siena every 30-60 minutes. It costs €9.10 single (Dec 2017). From the south, direct connections to Siena depart from Chiusior from Grosseto. The train station in Siena is located approximately 2 km from Siena's historical centre (follow directions "bus centro", you have to enter the mall to find the bus station to the city center), a five minute bus ride - buses leave regularly from Piazza del Sale. Buses numbers 3, 8, 10, 17, 77 leave from the station to Piazza del Sale and bus #17 departs from Piazza del Sale for the train station. If you don't mind walking uphill, you can also walk to the centre in about 20-30 minutes: Exit the train station, turn left, walk past the bus park and then uphill, bearing right at the traffic circle, staying on the road called Viale Giuseppe Manzini. Go through the city walls, and follow the road as it bends sharply to the right. The road becomes Via Garibaldi, which will take you into the city.

By bus
By far the easiest way to get to Siena from Florence (though the train journey is much more picturesque). Take the SITA bus (located in a small underground bus depot across the street, to the west of Santa Maria Novella train station). After 1hr 20 minutes it will arrive at the bus terminal at Piazza Antonio

Gramsci which is located well within the walls of the city, allowing for an easy walk to any of the city's attractions. The cost is €7.80 (May 2014) or €12.00 if you pay on board.

Connections are also available from Rome (3 hours) and various other cities.

To Get around
By car
The centre of Siena is accessible only on foot. Cars (other than taxis, police, etc.) are strictly prohibited; motorcycles and scooters are OK, though. Patrons of the central hotels are allowed to drive up and unload the luggage (and then get out), but only by obtaining one-time permission slips from the hotel front desk beforehand (also have them draw the route for you on a map and follow it to the letter; if you miss a turn, it may be wiser to head out the nearest gate, get on the circumferential road just outside the walls, return to the starting point and try again); have this pass handy if stopped by police while driving within the walls - or, in a pinch, at least a confirmation of your reservation. Don't rush your turns, and swing wide like a truck, as you would be sometimes required to fit between two stone walls into an opening just slightly wider

than your vehicle. Outside the main city walls can be found various parking areas. For more information, contact "Siena Parcheggi" tel. 0577-228711. To call or reserve a taxi, telephone the Central Reservation Office at 0577-49222.

Siena may be the only city in Mediterranean Europe where parking is not a massive headache, though charges have increased dramatically in the past few years and you can expect to pay €40,00 or more per day for the more convenient spots. The huge parking lots around the Fortezza and the adjacent football stadium are no longer free, but on the other hand, you can now count on finding a space there almost anytime; there is free parking further out, with minibus service, from Due Ponti and Coroncina (beyond Porta Romana).

By bus
Google maps shows the location of all bus stops within the city. If you zoom in and click the bus symbol on the map, you will get a list of bus routes serving that stop. There are several small buses (Pollicino) that cover some streets located in the centre and several bus lines to and from the outskirts of town. Bus tickets cost 1,50 € per fare when bought at kiosks/tabacchi but are more expensive when bought from the driver.

The site for Siena Mobilità wwwsienamobilita.it has bus schedules. Look for *orari*, then *orario invernale* (winter) or *orario estivo* (summer).: the Pollicini routes, the main urban routes, suburban routes, and the regional network including Florence and Pisa.

On foot
Siena is a city (a small city, yes, but it isn't like one of the hill towns) and the attractions away from the Piazza/Duomo area are spread out on three steep hills, so walking is a necessity. You will understand why Italians can eat so much, and not get fat, when you see old women carrying groceries up a long street with a 30-degree incline. If you are tired, check to see if you can get to your destination by walking along a ridge, rather than going in a straight line down a hill and back up.

Weather In Siena

To talk of the 'weather in Tuscany' is to generalise somewhat. Tuscany encompasses many diverse terrains and landscapes and the rules change from one zone to the next. You can be sure that July and August in Tuscany will be hot, sometimes stiflingly so, thanks to the humidity levels that can make Florence and the major cities of Tuscany veritable hothouses.

This situation is supposed to break around the day of feragosto in the middle of August, when the first rains are expected and with them a beginning of a decrease in temperature. September can still be very hot with October being a fine month to visit Tuscany - blue skies without the packed cities and the intense heat. But, some like it hot! November sees night-time temperatures really begin to drop, with crisp Autumn days to accompany the main olive harvest throughout Tuscany. Winter in Tuscany can be cold and wet but spring always seems to come quickly. March is azalea and camelia time, whilst April and May are sometimes very wet months.

Shopping in Siena

Italy is known throughout the world for its flair for fashion and design, and you can visit some of the most unique and memorable shops during your stay in Siena. You can find boutiques for clothing, shoes, gourmet food products, wine, housewares, framed art, artigianal paper, bookshops, and many other specialty items.

Siena is filled with one of a kind boutiques and shops at every corner, but you'll want to stroll along three main pedestrian streets for sure: Via di Citta, Banchi di Sopra and Via Dei

Montanini. Styles range from trendy to classic. You'll find a gelateria, pizza shop or bar between every few shops , so you can stop for gelato breaks between browsing.

Just window shopping in Siena can be enjoyable. Italians often stroll along the main streets, admiring the window displays and designs. Shopping in Siena is a great pleasure, and for the most part, Italian shopkeepers and sales help are extremely professional and polished - offering their advice on how to wear certain styles, what styles or colors suit you, or what the latest trends are. You can expect a high standard of personalized sales help, and shop owners who often do the buying personally.

You can shop for bargains in July and Febrary, the two times of the year when most shops reduce prices from 20% to 50% or more. Prices of items are reduced in the summer, in order to make room for the new fall and winter collections. They are reduced in February to make room for Spring collections.

Besides shops, there is an open air market held at the La Lizza (at the Fortezza) every Wednesday from 8 AM to around 1 PM. You can find stylish clothing, housewares or "do as the Italians do," and shop for fruits, vegetables and Italian cheeses.

Antiques

The best antiques shop in town is the Antichità Monna Agnese (tel. 0577-282-288), with a main branch at Via di Città 60 and another across the street at no. 45 that specializes in jewelry. There is also an outdoor antique market on the third Sunday every month at Piazza del Mercato.

Books & Paper

Feltrinelli, with store entrances at Via Banchi di Sopra 52 and 64-66 (tel. 0577-271-104 or 0577-44-009). For art and coffee-table books, often at a discount, hit Arte & Libri, Via di Città 111 (tel. 0577-221-325). If you enjoy browsing used books and old Italian postcards, you can check out Libreria Siena e Dintorni, a small second hand shop, tucked away on Via Provenzano Salvani, 8-10. You can find authentic Sienese and Florentine paper in Siena's fine paper shops.

The Siena branch of Florence's Il Papiro, Via di Città 37 (tel. 0577-284-241), carries fine stationery, marbelized paper products, and handcrafted journals. For more hand-made specialty papers, photo albums, recipe journals original paper designs from the Libreria Piccolomini Siena's Duomo, stop in La Stamperia, located at Via delle Terme, 80 (tel. 0577-280-443).

Many foreigners have their business cards made here, as the printing and paper selection are of a high quality, and the work is done at better prices than back home.

Ceramics and Housewares

The work of Ceramiche Artistiche Santa Caterina, with showrooms at Via di Città 51, 74, and 76 (tel. 0577-283-098) and a workshop outside town at Via P.A. Mattioli 12 (tel. 0577-45-006), are of good quality. Maestro Marcello Neri trained at Siena's art school and in the ceramics workshops of Montelupo Fiorentino, Tuscany's foremost ceramics center, before taking over this studio in 1961, aided by his talented wife, Franca Franci, and now their adult son, Fabio, also an art school grad. Look especially for their wares painted in "Sienese style" using only black, white, and *terra di Siena* reddish brown (what we call burnt sienna) with designs inspired by the oldest pavement panels in the Duomo. Most of the ceramics found in the shops of Via di Città, are of a souvenir quality.

Muzzi Sergio, Via dei Termini 97 (tel. 0577-40-439), is a friendly designer housewares shop, perfect for that set of grappa glasses or Alessi kitchen gadget.

Clothing, Shoes And Leather

Italy's high fashion designers such as Armani, Gucci, Versace, Burberry, Missoni -- and some more affordable labels too, can be found at Cortecci, Via Banchi di Sopra 27 (tel. 0577-280-096. There's also a branch on Il Campo at 30-31 (tel. 0577-280-984).

Ginger is a boutique with trendy Italian styled separates for women. If you follow the steps behind the Duomo, you will soon arrive on Via del Pellegrini, where Ginger is located. Something bought at Ginger is always remembered, but be prepared to spend a pretty penny.

For something a bit more unique, drop by Fioretta Bacci and her pair of giant looms taking up most of the room at Tessuti a Mano, Via San Pietro 7 (tel. 0577-282-200). Fioreta weaves all her incredible scarves, shawls, and sweaters by hand.

Fabrics and linens, both as raw materials and made into sheets, curtains, or embroidered hand towels, are the stock in trade of Debora Loreni's Antiche Dimore, Via di Città< 115 (tel. 0577-45-337). Signora Bruna Brizi Fontani is a bundle of energy and full of stories in her little embroidery and needlepoint store, Siena Ricama, Via di Città 61 (tel. 0577-288-339). She spends so much time chatting with visitors in her workroom and shopit is hard to believe she can finish the wonderful lampshades and other objects -- every one stitched by Fontani herself. They're inspired by medieval Sienese art: the Duomo floor, illuminated manuscripts, the frescoes of the Lorenzetti brothers, and anything else that catches her fancy from art history books and local museums.

FOOD, WINE & SWEETS

Those with a passion for la cucina italiana will not want to miss a stop in the Antica Drogheria Manganelli, Via di Città 71-73 (tel. 0577-280-002), since 1879 making its own panforte (one of the few left) and delicious soft *ricciarelli* almond cookies. It also carries the tops in Tuscan products, like vinegar from Castello di Volpaia and cured meats from Greve in Chianti's Falorni butchers.

For less touristy (and cheaper) pickings of traditional regional foods, head to one of the spots where many Sienese come to stock up. La Terra di Siena, Via G. Dupré 32 (tel. 0577-223-528), looks like a bargain basement-type place with stacks of regional products like Sienese cookies and area wines, honeys, cheeses, and meats, but it actually carries quality merchandise (at great prices).

The supermarket-like Consorzio Agrario Siena, Via Piangiani 9 (tel. 0577-2301), has been a farmer's co-op since 1901; it offers a nice selection of meats, cheeses, pasta, cookies by Tuscan producers.

SWEETS

Siena is famous for its delectable variety of cakes and cookies made with recipes dating from medieval times. Sienese sweets include *cavallucci* (sweet spice biscuits), *panforte* (once enjoyed as a traditional holiday dessert, has now become a year-round pleasure for visitors to Siena), made with honey, hazelnuts, almonds, and a secret blend of spices which includes cinammon and nutmeg), *ricciarelli* (almond-paste cookies), and *castagnaccio* (baked in the fall and winter - a batter of chestnut flour, topped with pine nuts and rosemary).

For a taste of some of Siena's best pastries, head for Pasticceria Bini behind the left flank of the Duomo at Via dei Fusari 9-13 (tel. 0577-280-207), where since 1943 they've filled the neighborhood with the aroma of Siena's dolci. They still make their delicious sweets on-site -- you can watch them at work through the next window down the street. Be sure to try the Forno Le Campane on Via di Citta' also.

Pasticceria Nannini is Siena's oldest pasticceria, and has a main branch on Via Banchi di Sopra 22-24.

Sports In Siena

Sports, Physical Fitness And Recreation In Siena
Siena is filled with sports and recreational activities. Some sports are soccer, basketball, tennis, archery, horseback riding, cycling, golf and swimming. There are many fitness centers, gyms and public sports facilities located in Siena.

Soccer

Siena Football Team
Siena's soccer team is a series A team, and the stadium is located in the city centre next to piazza San Domenico. Stadio Artemio Franchi, Via dello Stadio 3. Check the page on Siena football club for more information on the team.

Siena football team was born thanks to the activity of a youths' group who decided to break with the sport club they belonged to (the so called Mens Sana in Corpore Sano sport club) to make a new one contrasting with the previous idea. The new club took the name of Società Studio e Divertimento (Study and Fun sport club) before (1904) and then it was called Società Sportiva Robur (Robur sport club) at the entrance of football game in the Italian sport field (it was imported from America), in 1908. In 1921 the Robur football team started to take part in the official championship gaining an important advancement. The social colour of the team already was black and white-striped. In 1930s Robur was one of the most organized Tuscan sport clubs and in 1933/34 they changed again their name in Associazione Calcio Siena (Siena football club). The new Siena football team reached the serie B (the second Italian division) twice, in 1935 and in 1937/38; actually in that last season the opening of the new stadium was made (it was 8 of December 1938) and it took the name of "Rino Dauss" stadium (its name changed twice in the following years: it was called "Rastrello" and then it took the final and current name of "Artemio Franchi" stadium).

The Siena football team reached some significant winning posts during the following years, as well as important wins versus Fiorentina and Bologna (two of the most influential Italian football teams of that time), but its run was interrupted by the unhappy event of the second world war. From 1945/46 season the club had to deal with a long series of vicissitudes making it continuously oscillate from serie B to serie C (the third Italian division) and also to lower categories, as long as a new young president, Danilo Nannini, came to raise again the fortune of the team (it was in the mid of 1950s). He made a big effort and tought out different devices to save them, even if the real issue of Siena football club was money: it wasn't rich enough to compete with the biggest Italian clubs. At the end of 1960s they were in serie D and Mr Nannini left the team within an inch of flop. After a few years, he took it back (in '80s) making it able to get the serie C1 in 1981/82, then leaving again the direction to Mr Max Paganini, who made the history of Siena football team from that moment until 1997.

In 1997 Paganini gave the team to Mr Claudio Corradini (important name of the SNAI Services group).

n 1999 Siena finally gained the serie B under the training of Mr Sala (the so called 'coach of the rebirth') and after a few time, among the disputes of fans and sports men, all the quotas of the club ended up in Mr Paolo De Luca (who became the new president) and the Finanziaria Senese di Sviluppo's hands who made it grow into a serie A competitive team.

The club currently plays in Serie A, having gained promotion from Serie B at the end of the 2010-2011 season.

Swimming

There are several public swimming pools located in Siena. In addition to the area's public pool, some hotels offer the option to use their pool for a day of swimming, while enjoying the view of Siena.

Theaters In Siena

During the warm weather months, many live concerts, dance performances, theatrical performances, poetry readings and films are held outdoors -- against the backdrop of the unique architecture and history that Siena offers. The fortezza, Piazza del Campo and the ancient fountain at Via Fontebranda are a some of the unique locations that serve as outdoor theaters for performances in the spring, summer and fall.

During the late fall and winter, the many beautiful churches and oratorie are transformed with small intimate concerts that range from classical music to improvisational jazz. For theatrical performances during the winter months, the following indoor theaters offer a range of programs in Siena:

Dei Rinnovati
Inside the Town Hall you can find the "Teatro dei Rinnovati" where touring opera, dance and drama can be seen.

Address: Piazza del Campo, 1

Ticket Office Phone: 0577 292265

Site - More info:

Dei Rozzi

Teatro dei Rozzi in Piazza Indipendenza 15 has been recently restored and now offers a range of programs and performances.

Piccolo Teatro

Located in Via Montanini presents a small, local company. You have to inquire with the owners in advance in order to find out more information about the schedule of events.

Address: Via dei Montanini 118

Ticket Office Phone: 0577 281190

Salone dei Concerti at the Accademia Musicale Chigiana

The room - the largest in the palace - is used as a concert hall by the Accademia Musicale Chigiana. The décor is in the eighteenth-century Venetian style, with rocaille stuccoes and delicate shades of color.

Address: via di Città 89

Ticket Office Phone: 0577 22091

Nightlife In Siena

Even though Siena may seem like a quiet town, you can still find a variety of bars and pubs, to meet friends for a beer or glass of wine.

Much time is spent strolling from cafe to cafe, and gathering with friends at Piazza del Campo to listen to live music, watch performances by improvisational entertainers such as fire eaters and clowns, or just enjoying a gelato and the view. The Sienese enjoy the tradition of an evening walk, the "passeggiata", through Banchi di Sopra, while admiring the new window displays and socializing with friends and neighbors.

Below are a few of the pubs and places to frequent during the evening hours.

115 Bar

In via dei Rossi) It was first opened in 1979 in a 14th century palace, and is now furnished with souvenirs of the owner's journeys enjoy, in a quiet setting, dishes prepared in a superb kitchen. Open until about 2 a.m.

Al Cambio

In via Pantaneto) A late night spot for university students, sometimes has evening of live rock music, the bar serves all kind of drinks and is open until about 2 a.m., it gets lively late and on weekends.

Bar Porrione

In the same named street, via del Porrione, about 20 meters from Piazza del Campo, this bar is a hot spot in the nightlife of University students: people pop in for a cheap draught beer, a game of flipper and late night chat. open late until about 3 a.m.

Casa del Boia

(In Piazza del Mercato) This used to be the local executioner's house, and was connected to the execution site by an underground tunnel. It has been transformed into a popular night place, organizing special nights dedicated to, for example singles, foreigners, or cuban music.

Caffe del Corso

For staying out late, or for a cocktail, this bar/caffe offers it all. Located on Banchi di Sopra, the place is filled with young people. There is a nice offering of snacks downstairs and a small dance floor upstairs.

Il Barone Rosso

Food, beer and live music. It is in the centre, and can be found by walking through the streets around Piazza Independenza.

L'Officina

This is a local hangout in Piazza del Sale, with live music and DJ.

The Dublin Post

In Piazza Gramsci, this Irish pub has traditional Irish music from time to time, but also live music too, with a selection of Irish beers and a nice antipasti bar for happy hour.

Robert the Bruce

Near the Fortezza, on Via Monte Santo, this pub gets lively late at night, but offers a large selection of British beers, and fried food.

Enoteca Italiana

Located in the Fortezza, this wine bar offers many opportunities to taste and sample the local and not-so-local wine of Italy. It has a nice outdoor terrace, with tables where you can sit and sip your wine.

The Tea Rooms

Near Porta Giustizia, this comfortable place offers different teas, cocktails and alcoholic drinks accompanied by snacks. Occasionally they have live music, of the jazz variety.

For weekly theater performances, concerts, poetry readings and other evening events, look for advertisements posted on the walls of the main streets of Siena, on the doors of shops in the historical center, and in the tourism office.

During the season of the Palio, be sure to find out which contrada is having a festa each week. Each contrada has a particular week in which they have outdoor celebrations, with a dance floor, live bands, dinners in gardens, and special outdoor eating areas for gelato, pizza and grilled meats.

Quality Of Life In Siena

Siena boasts a very high quality of living, made possible by the unique location and history of the city. It is filled with charming architecture, the culture of art, nature, and offers a balance of active student life and tranquility.

It's location is unique in that you can be in the middle of the medieval center one moment, but you can walk for less than 30 minutes and find yourself in the middle of some of Italy's most enchanting countryside.

here are no factories and or industrial settlements of a noticeable size close to Siena, so air pollution is quite low. Also, because the city is surrounded by the countryside, and because the city authority has taken special care to ensure the city proper is off limits to many vehicles.

The culture and tradition of the city is evident in the Palio. The city is divided into "contrade," and there are advantages for the elderly, who have a community and social activities this way, and for the young people, who share social life in a rather small human scale, and therefore are less exposed to the dangers of drugs, alcohol and the like.

All the activities for the preparation of the Palio are an occasion for children, young people and elderly together to have something to do, on a voluntary basis, for a good part of the *summer months*.

Additional factors are, the quality of wine and food, and the favorable climate. There are several thermal springs and spas villages close to Siena, and the city is only about 1 hour away from the coastal area.

Events In Siena

more information on your arrival but below are a few things you may want to check out. Information and reservations for disabled persons for events organized by the City Administration Phone: 0577 292215.

Accademia Musicale Chigiana
The famous Accademia Musicale Chigiana on Via di Citta sponsors classical concerts and opera all year round, culminating in the Chigiana International Festival and Summer Academy in July and August. During this event the musicians perform in many theatres and historic palaces in the city.

Address: Accademia Musicale Chigiana, da Basso, Via di Città, 89

Phone: 0577 22091 / Fax: 0577 288 124

Operas In Monteriggioni Castle
A magic scenary for Verdi and Puccini's Operas: inside the Monteriggioni Castle!

Discover this wonderful event during summer, visit our page dedicated to Opera and Classical Concert in Monteriggioni!

Associazione Siena Jazz
In July/August the Siena Jazz Association organises many open-air concerts. In winter its activities are based on particular events and various professional courses.

Address: Fortezza Medicea, 10

Phone: 0577 271 401 / Fax: 0577 271 404

Outdoor Cinema & Theater
During the summer, the program "Cinema in Fortezza" shows outdoor movies at the Fortezza Medici in June and July. During the month of August, films are shown at some of the parks in Siena. A different movie is featured each night, under the stars. Also, outdoor theater performances by small community groups are sometimes offered. Look around for advertisements for small, inexpensive performances that are often posted around town.

Sagres & Festivals: Le Sagre E Le Feste
These small celebrations in communities in and surrounding Siena, and also held in the contrade of Siena are usually held during Spring, Summer and Fall. The Sagra celebrates a particular food product or type of local specialty, and festivals range from political to religious. Festivals range from "Festa dell'Uva"(Chianciano Terme), to "Sagra della Bruschetta"(Gaiole in Chianti), to "Sagra del Fungo." Contact the office of tourism for an updated schedule.

Treno Natura

Treno Natura is a relaxed train trip through the countryside south of Siena, from spring to autumn, these old-style trains depart on Sundays for the day through the Val d'Arbia, Val d'Orcia and La Crete. For those of you who interested in exploring the magnificent Siena countryside in all its grandeur and tranquillity, take a ride on the Natura Train. This seasonal adventure on a steam powered train takes you back to "another time" with its winding paths through the Sienese countryside. The trip begins in Siena and stops in Asciano and Monte Antico before returning to Siena.

Phone: 0577 207413

Markets
There's an extensive city market every Wednesday between 8am and 1pm, filling the streets around the Fortezza and La Lizza park. An antique market takes place in Piazza del Mercato on the 3rd Sunday of every month, except in August.

Two sample festivals during the year are: Santa Lucia, December 13, Pian dei Mantellini and San Giuseppe, March 19, Contrada dell'Onda, Via Duprè

Etruscans Of Siena

Although there is still some debate over the origins of Siena, is was most likely founded by Etruscans. Experts have different opinions on the exact origins of the Etruscans, but it is said that they migrated from the Aegeo-Asian area at the end of the 12th Century BC. The Etruscans were hilltop dwellers, and every hill had its own farmhouse just as we can still see today in the countryside around Siena.

The Etruscans had a most fascinating sub-terranean culture. Their belief in the afterlife, made it important to bury the dead with everything they might need for life after death. In Chiusi, a maze of underground tunnels is believed to have housed the mythical tomb of King Porsenna. Chiusi's underground tunnels contain an extraordinary storehouse of names bearing similarities with surnames still in use nowadays, and the Etruscan heritage is still found as an influence in the cuisine, and even in the DNA of the local population.

A sample group of residents of the town of MURLO have been tested for their genetic makeup, in order to find out possible genetic connections with their Etruscan forebears: comparison with the DNA extracted from bones from the tombs will definitely confirm if these people may still consider themselves "Etruscans".

The Chiusi Etruscan museum, and other Etruscans sites are within easy reach in the area around Siena, such as Chianti, Val di Merse and throughout the province in many museums.

Museum Info:
Museo Archeologico

Archeological Museum in Murlo

Address: Piazza della Cattedrale (MURLO)

Museo Archeologico Nazionale
National Archeological Museum that also organizes visits to the Etruscan tombs.
Address: Via Porsenna, 17 (CHIUSI)

Also, not far from Siena, the Etruscans had the city-state of Volaterrae, which is now known as Volterra. An excellent Etruscan museum can be visited there.

Museo Etrusco Guarnacci: There are 600 funerary urns on exhibit here, in addition to many other fascinating exhibits of local Etruscan finds.

Roman Reynolds

The End

Made in United States
Orlando, FL
24 December 2022